STORMSCA

LANDSCAPING TO MINIMIZE WIND DAMAGE IN FLORIDA

Pamela Crawford

The Breakers Hotel in Palm Beach one month after it was hit by Frances and Jeanne.
These plants, including the Phoenix dactylifera palms, are obviously quite wind-tolerant!

Color Garden, Inc.

Copyright

Published by Color Garden, Inc., 5596 Western Way, Lake Worth, FL 33463, 561-964-6500, www.easygardencolor.com

First printing: 2005

Library of Congress Catalog Card Number pending

ISBN number 0-9712220-2-9

Purchasing Information

The book is available through most booksellers and many garden centers in Florida. It is also available through Amazon.com for orders from out of state. To locate your nearest source or order wholesale, contact Color Garden.

Color Garden
5596 Western Way
Lake Worth, FL 33463
Phone: 561-964-6500 Cell (Pamela Crawford): 561-371-2719
Email: colorgdn@aol.com
Web site: www.easygardencolor.com

Credits

Author: Pamela Crawford
Research Assistant: Barbara Hadsell. She also wrote pages 96 and 97.
Proofreader: Barbara Iderosa, Best Editing Service, Wellington, Florida
Computer Consulting: Roger Rosenthal, Affordable Computer Training, Palm Beach Gardens, Florida
Photos are by Pamela Crawford or otherwise notated in the caption. Cover photos: Front cover house, FEMA; hurricane graphic, FEMA.
Credits for maps and graphics are given on the pages the work is shown.
Cover Design: Katie Deitz

Contents

Chapter 1
UNDERSTAND HURRICANE BASICS
Page 10

Chapter 2
KNOW YOUR PLANT'S WIND TOLERANCE
Page 28

Chapter 3
OTHER REASONS WHY TREES FALL
Page 92

Chapter 4
DESIGNING TO MINIMIZE WIND DAMAGE
Page 106

Chapter 5
PROPER STORM AFTERCARE
Page 122

Contributors

Janet Alford, Director, McKee Botanical Gardens, Vero Beach, FL
John Atkins, Extension Agent-Agriculture/Livestock, UF/IFAS Santa Rosa County Extension
Beth Bolles, Extension Agent, Horticulture specialist, UF/IFAS Escambia County Extension
Robert Bowden, Director, Harry P. Leu Botanical Gardens, Orlando
Pam Brown, Urban Horticulture Agent, UF/IFAS Pinellas County Extension
Stephen Brown, Horticulture Agent, UF/IFAS Lee County Extension
Jim Burch, Supervisory Botanist, Resource Management Office, Big Cypress National Preserve, Ochopee
Doug Caldwell, Horticulture Agent, UF/IFAS Collier County Extension
Greg Cotton, Road Inspection Supervisor, Santa Rosa County Public Works Dept.
Daniel F. Culbert, Extension Agent III, Environmental Horticulture, UF/IFAS Okeechobee County Extension
Jackie Dawson
Peggy Dessaint, Extension Agent, Commercial Landscape Horticulture, UF/IFAS, Manatee County Extension
District X of the Florida Federation of Garden Clubs
Butch DuCote, FEMA Public Affairs Officer
Mary L. Duryea, Ph.D., Assist. Dean for Research & Assist. Director, FL Agricultural Experiment Station, Institute of Food &
Agricultural Sciences
James Evans, Environmental Planner, Department of Natural Resources, City of Sanibel
Florida Native Plant Society, Palm Beach Chapter
Theresa Friday, Extension Agent, UF/IFAS Santa Rosa County Extension
Steve Graham, Tampa Municipal Forester
Carol Hall, FFGC 3rd Vice President, Florida Federation of Garden Clubs, Palm Beach Gardens
Roger Hammer, Naturalist and Director, Castellow Hammock Nature Center
Adrian Hunsberger, M.S., Urban Horticulture Agent, Entomologist, Master Gardener Coordinator, UF/IFAS Miami-Dade Co. Extension
Rusty Isler, MCSE, Information Services Manager, The Island Water Association, Inc.
Suzi James, Heathcote Botanical Gardens Inc., Fort Pierce
Rick Joyce, Director, Department of Community Development, Lee County Division of Environmental Sciences
Chris Lockhart, Plant Ecologist, Habitat Specialists, Inc. Boynton Beach, FL
Robert K. Loflin, Ph.D., Natural Resources Director, City of Sanibel
Jim Lushine, Warning Coordination Meteorologist, National Weather Service, Weather Service Forecast Office
Tom MacCubbin, Extension Agent IV, UF/IFAS, Orange County Extension
Carol Martin
Max Mayfield, Director, National Hurricane Center
Kelly Mikesell
Ralph Mitchell, Director UF/IFAS Charlotte County Extension Service
Jim Moll, Urban Horticulture Extension Agent, UF/IFAS, Hernando County Extension
Louise Moor
Dan Mullins, County Agent, UF/IFAS Santa Rosa County Extension
William O'Brien, Director of Emergency Operations, Palm Beach County
Mark Peters, Director of Horticulture, McKee Botanical Garden, Vero Beach
Rusty Pfost, Meteorologist-in-Charge, Weather Forecast Office, National Weather Service
Wendy Poag, Florida Native Plant Society, Beautyberry Chapter, Lake County
Bill Reeves, Botanical Visions, Boca Raton, Florida
Sally Scalera, Brevard County Extension Agent
Linda Seals, University of Florida Master Gardener Program, Mounts Botanical Garden, West Palm Beach
Sheila Seme
Holly Shackelford, Horticulture Program Coordinator, Charlotte County Extension Service
Shadetree Services, Stuart
Mary Steward
Cindy Turner, Bok Sanctuary, Lake Wales
Don Wacker
Teresa Watkins, Florida Yards and Neighborhoods, UF/IFAS Lake, Orange, & Seminole County Extension
Bill Whiting, Web editor, Florida Power and Light
Larry Williams Extension Agent, UF/IFAS Okaloosa County Extension
Sherry Williams, AICP, Special Projects Coordinator, Brevard County Natural Resources Management Office
Zimmerman Tree Service, Palm Beach County

Climate and Zone Information

Range of this book: This book covers the state of Florida, which includes zones 8, 9, 10, and 11. "South Florida" refers to zones 10 and 11. "Central Florida" is zone 9, and "North Florida" is zone 8.

The Truth about Zone Hardiness Maps: I used to think that the zone maps were always right. Not so! **The Zone Hardiness Maps are more of a 'be careful' than a 'do not plant in your zone or it will quickly die.'** And, it's not as easy as the zone map makes it look. Technically, a zone map would look like a Doppler Radar screen, with zones 9 and 10 being mixed up all over Tampa. Many zone 10 plants are traditionally planted all over central Florida, which is zone 9. Bromeliads and Hibiscus are good examples. Both are quite common in Tampa and Orlando, which is zone 9. The Bromeliad Society was even founded in Orlando, where Bromeliads are not supposed to survive the winters! (Since Bromeliads like shade, most are planted under trees, which usually gives the necessary protection from the cold.) **The individual plants in this book are classed by USDA zone _as well as local use patterns._**

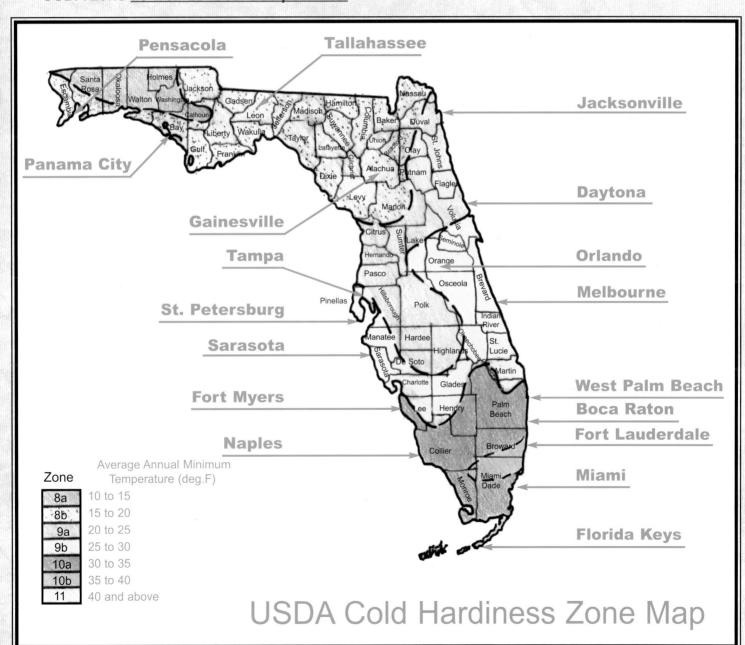

Zone	Average Annual Minimum Temperature (deg.F)
8a	10 to 15
8b	15 to 20
9a	20 to 25
9b	25 to 30
10a	30 to 35
10b	35 to 40
11	40 and above

USDA Cold Hardiness Zone Map

Author's Notes

Background: I began gardening at age 3 with my English mother in Mississippi. I moved to Florida in the 70's, planning to have a gorgeous garden filled with color. The next few years brought more blunders than blooms, as I made every gardening mistake in the book! These early errors started a three-decade saga to learn everything I could about Florida gardening. I received a Master's Degree in Landscape Architecture from Florida International University, followed by starting a nursery and garden design business. While designing 1500 gardens, I also started my own trial gardens (on the eight acres where I live and work) to determine which Florida plants gave the highest performance with the least amount of care. Of the thousands of plants tested to date, only about 300 lived through my difficult trials in my low-maintenance gardens. These are truly tough plants!

I am now writing a series of books called the "Florida Gardening Series" about my trial garden experiences. The first volume, "Easy Gardens for South Florida," was published in 2001 and features 100 easy plants as well as all you ever needed to know about how to plant and maintain your Florida garden. It will be revised soon to cover all of Florida, and the title will change to "Easy Gardens for Florida." "Best Garden Color for Florida" is the second volume. It covers everything you ever wanted to know about Florida garden color. This book, "StormScaping," is the third volume.

Above left: (l-r) Barbara Hadsell, researcher; Max Mayfield, director of the National Hurricane Center; and Pamela Crawford, the author Photo by Bill O'Brien. Right: (l-r) Barbara Hadsell at the National Weather Service with Jim Lushine and Rusty Pfost.

Writing this Book: After Hurricane Andrew, I researched the wind tolerance of many plants. I included the wind tolerance of every plant I could find information on in the individual plant profiles of my first two books. I also included chapters on dealing with salt and wind.

Frances and Jeanne were my first hurricanes. We were clobbered. My nursery and beautiful trial gardens were in shambles. But in the course of the clean up, I realized that one of my gardens was almost completely untouched - just like the storms had never happened. I call this garden my "survivor garden" and tell its secrets in chapter 3. It was my first inspiration to write this book. I wanted to share information about how to protect gardens from wind.

As I began to see the destruction throughout Florida, I realized that a lot of it could have been prevented. Many trees that are not tolerant of wind are planted near power lines and buildings. It was definitely time for a new book!

I realized that, for first time, we had a lot of available data on plant's wind tolerance. Had I been able to hire about a thousand scientists, I would have had them traveling around Florida counting trees, using scientific methods to give us definitive information on every plant species that grows inside our borders. However, since I just had myself and Barbara Hadsell to do the research, we reached out to experts and homeowners alike to gather what information we could share with you.

Author's Notes and Glossary

We had a great response to our inquiries, particularly from county extension agents in the areas that were hurt the worse by the 2004 storms. The botanical gardens of the state were also quite generous with information and photos. The Florida Native Plant Society from Palm Beach County shared a survey that included invaluable information.

Barbara and I traveled to all the areas where the hurricanes made landfall, photographing and interviewing as we went. I would particularly like to thank Barbara for her untiring dedication to this project. And her husband Tim, who nicknamed her "Hurricane Hadsell"!

We met with emergency managers and the weather experts at the National Hurricane Center as well. We emailed our reader list and received a lot of great information from homeowners around the state.

And we emailed a lot of people with a lot of questions, continually for months. I would like to thank each and every one of our contributors, listed on page four, for their patience, advice, and time they spent on this project.

Much of this information is not scientific, but anecdotal, meaning information that is passed from person to person, mostly by word of mouth or email. Although it's not perfect, it's a start. I look forward to this book evolving through the years as more people give me information about their observations of a plants' wind tolerance.

And we found answers that can help us weather the coming windy years!

Above, left: Barbara Hadsell, researcher and Bill O'Brien, Director of Emergency Operations for Palm Beach County. Right: Miguel Olivares-Popoca, manager of the Color Garden nursery and trial gardens.

Glossary

Wind Tolerance: **Very high wind tolerance:** Plants that hold together fairly well in cat 1 to cat 4 hurricanes; some of the plants in this category, like the pygmy date palm, do fairly well in cat 5 storms as well. I classified very few plants with this wind tolerance, probably underestimating the strength of some plants for dealing with these high winds. I felt it best to err on the side of caution with a study as anecdotal as this one. **High wind tolerance:** Plants that hold together pretty well in hurricanes from cat 1 to cat 3. They may not die in stronger hurricanes, but will be pretty torn up. **Medium wind tolerance:** Plants that hold together fairly well in cat 1 and cat 2 storms. They may not die in stronger hurricanes, but will be pretty torn up. **Low wind tolerance:** Plants that routinely show damage in cat 1 storms. They may not die in stronger hurricanes, but will be pretty torn up. Not all of them show damage, but a significant percentage of them will not fare very well.

The Most Important Lessons...

Go outside and look at all of your trees. Write down their names. If you don't know their names, take photos of them to your county extension office to identify. Go to http://extadmin.ifas.ufl.edu/Extlinks.htm to find the address and phone number of your local county extension. Then, look them up in this book and find out how wind tolerant they are. If they pose a danger to your house, consider removing them. Be sure to check with your county or city regarding tree removal permits.

Don't let one tree destroy your home, or you may end up like John Atkins and his family. <u>One tree</u> fell on their house during Ivan and ruined it. They moved in with relatives and four of them shared a room for two months until they could rent a single-wide trailer. They will stay there for another year or two until their new house is ready. All of this financial and emotional stress for just one tree! See their story on page 52.

Don't think that all trees that are close to houses fall on them. Look at the lessons from Sanibel, the astounding discovery of Dr. Robert Loflin, Natural Resources Director, City of Sanibel. He states that houses in Sanibel that were ravaged by Hurricane Charley fared better with certain kinds of trees around them! So, some trees actually can protect your home rather than destroy it. But, you must have the knowledge that you will find in Chapters 2 and 3 to know what kind of trees and how to arrange them. And the knowledge from Chapter 1 explains how a small percentage of hurricanes will knock down any tree, except maybe for the pygmy date palm!

In This Book

The Six Most Expensive Landscape Mistakes

1. Not knowing the wind tolerance of your plants.
See Chapter 2 for detailed information. Don't make the common mistake of thinking that if your tree did not fall in Charley, Jeanne, Frances, or Ivan, that it will stand in the next storm. The next storm could be stronger, or the wind could come from another direction. See what the experts say in Chapter 2 before deciding to remove any trees.

2. Neglecting routine tree trimming.
See Chapter 3 for the latest on proper tree-trimming practices.

3. Bad trimming after the storm.
See Chapter 5 for guidelines on trimming your trees after the storm.

4. After the storm, throwing away valuable trees that could have easily been saved.

5. Planting large trees near power lines.
See Chapter 3 for FPL guidelines.

6. Planting wind-sensitive trees near buildings.

Chapter 1
Understand Hurricane Basics:
When are they coming?
What will they do to us?

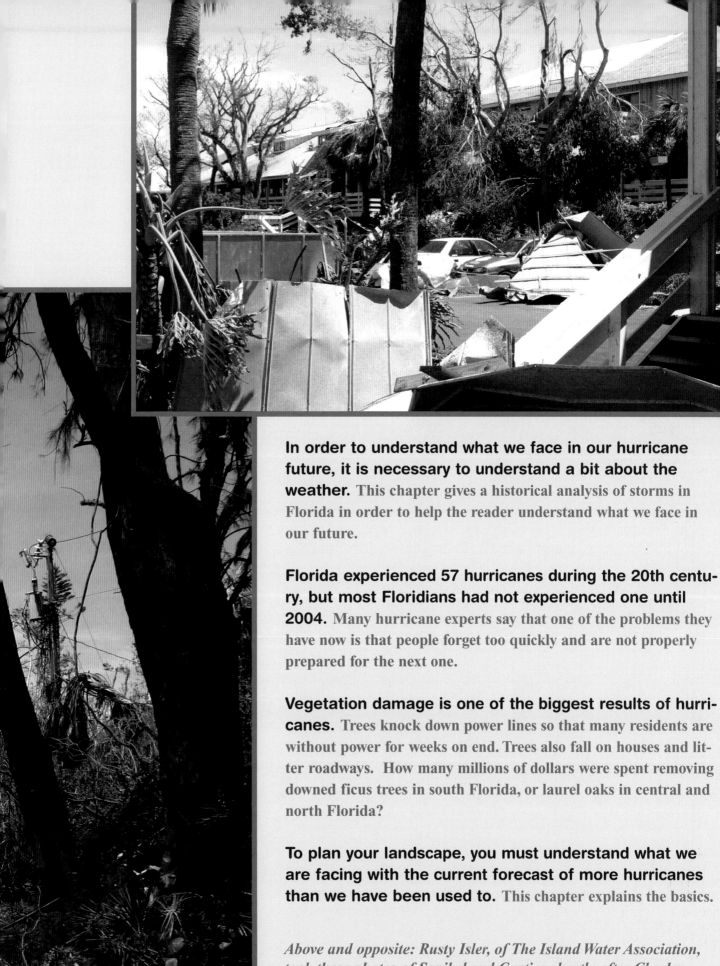

In order to understand what we face in our hurricane future, it is necessary to understand a bit about the weather. This chapter gives a historical analysis of storms in Florida in order to help the reader understand what we face in our future.

Florida experienced 57 hurricanes during the 20th century, but most Floridians had not experienced one until 2004. Many hurricane experts say that one of the problems they have now is that people forget too quickly and are not properly prepared for the next one.

Vegetation damage is one of the biggest results of hurricanes. Trees knock down power lines so that many residents are without power for weeks on end. Trees also fall on houses and litter roadways. How many millions of dollars were spent removing downed ficus trees in south Florida, or laurel oaks in central and north Florida?

To plan your landscape, you must understand what we are facing with the current forecast of more hurricanes than we have been used to. This chapter explains the basics.

Above and opposite: Rusty Isler, of The Island Water Association, took these photos of Sanibel and Captiva shortly after Charley.

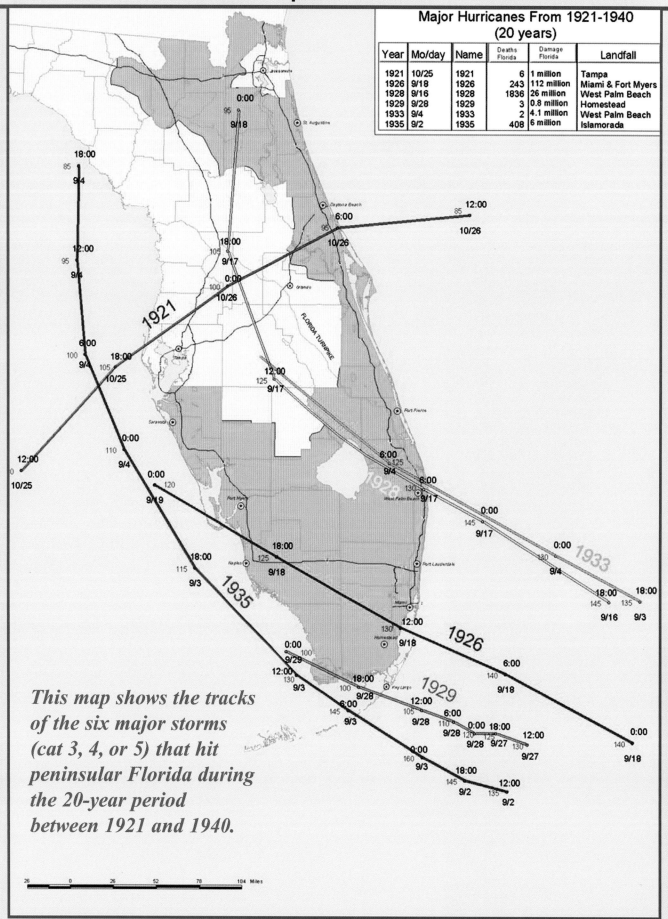

Major Hurricanes From 1921-1940 (20 years)					
Year	Mo/day	Name	Deaths Florida	Damage Florida	Landfall
1921	10/25	1921	6	1 million	Tampa
1926	9/18	1926	243	112 million	Miami & Fort Myers
1928	9/16	1928	1836	26 million	West Palm Beach
1929	9/28	1929	3	0.8 million	Homestead
1933	9/4	1933	2	4.1 million	West Palm Beach
1935	9/2	1935	408	6 million	Islamorada

This map shows the tracks of the six major storms (cat 3, 4, or 5) that hit peninsular Florida during the 20-year period between 1921 and 1940.

14 major (cat 3-5) hurricanes

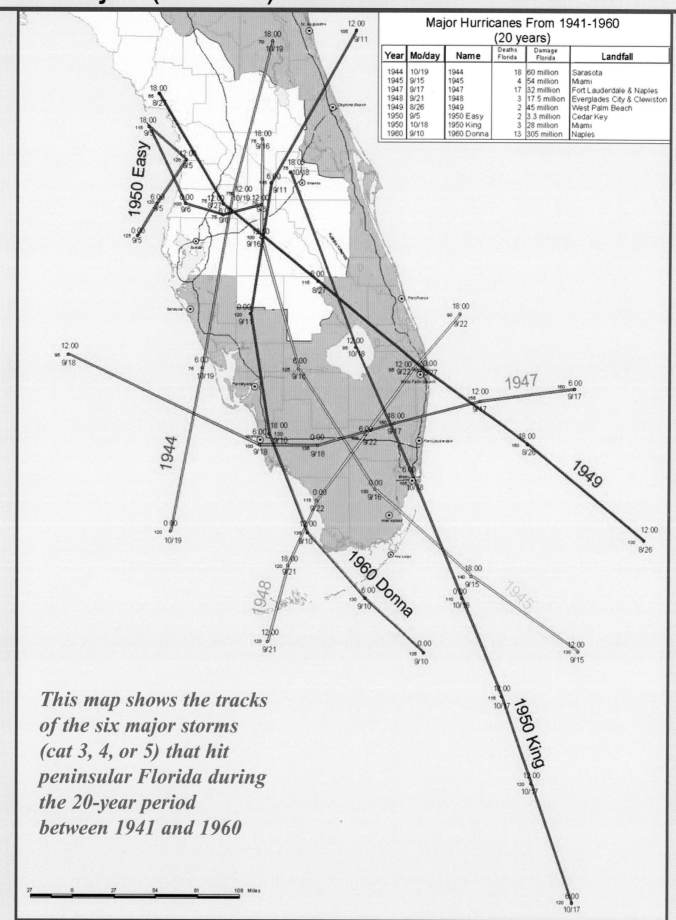

Major Hurricanes From 1941-1960 (20 years)					
Year	Mo/day	Name	Deaths Florida	Damage Florida	Landfall
1944	10/19	1944	18	60 million	Sarasota
1945	9/15	1945	4	54 million	Miami
1947	9/17	1947	17	32 million	Fort Lauderdale & Naples
1948	9/21	1948	3	17.5 million	Everglades City & Clewiston
1949	8/26	1949	2	45 million	West Palm Beach
1950	9/5	1950 Easy	2	3.3 million	Cedar Key
1950	10/18	1950 King	3	28 million	Miami
1960	9/10	1960 Donna	13	305 million	Naples

This map shows the tracks of the six major storms (cat 3, 4, or 5) that hit peninsular Florida during the 20-year period between 1941 and 1960

Hurricanes come in spurts, as shown by these three maps of cat 3,4, and 5 storms that hit peninsular Florida (not including the panhandle) during an eighty-year period (see previous two pages to see other two maps).

The previous pages show that **fourteen** major hurricanes hit peninsular Florida during the forty-year period from 1921 to 1960.

The opposite page shows that just **two** major storms hit peninsular Florida during the next forty-year period.

Imagine combining all the tracking lines you see on both of the maps on the previous pages added together on the map opposite, and you'll get an idea of just how good we had it from 1961 to 2000.

Times have changed. We are back in a hurricane-prevalent weather period like that from 1921 to 1960.

And these maps don't even include cat 1 or 2 storms, which we know can wreak havoc with vegetation.

peninsular Florida had 2 major (cat 3-5) hurricanes.

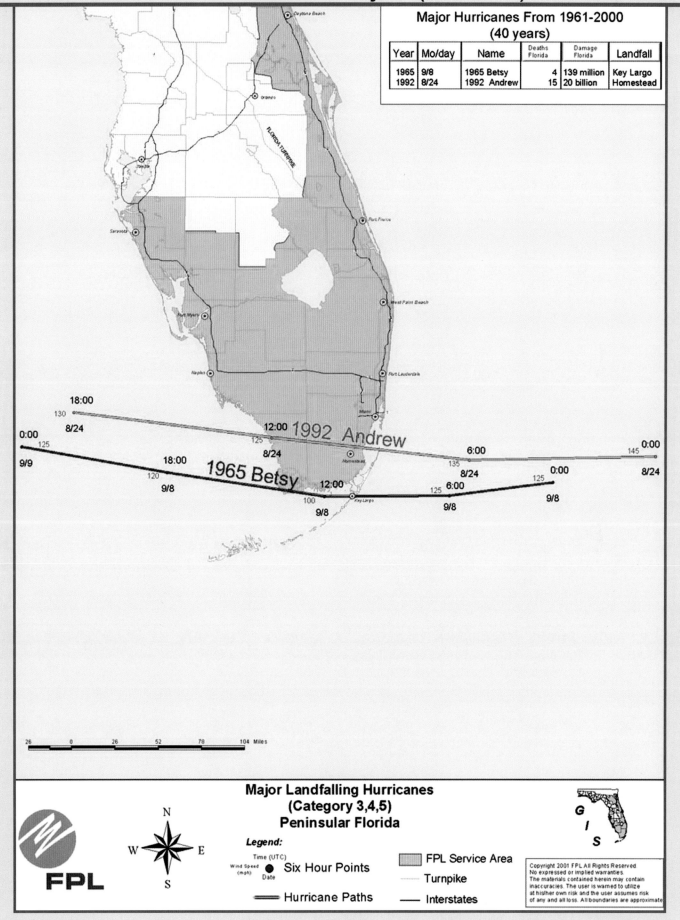

Major Hurricanes From 1961-2000
(40 years)

Year	Mo/day	Name	Deaths Florida	Damage Florida	Landfall
1965	9/8	1965 Betsy	4	139 million	Key Largo
1992	8/24	1992 Andrew	15	20 billion	Homestead

Major Landfalling Hurricanes
(Category 3,4,5)
Peninsular Florida

Legend:

Six Hour Points

Hurricane Paths

FPL Service Area

Turnpike

Interstates

The Hurricanes of 2004...

Hurricane Jeanne makes landfall near Port Saint Lucie, Florida

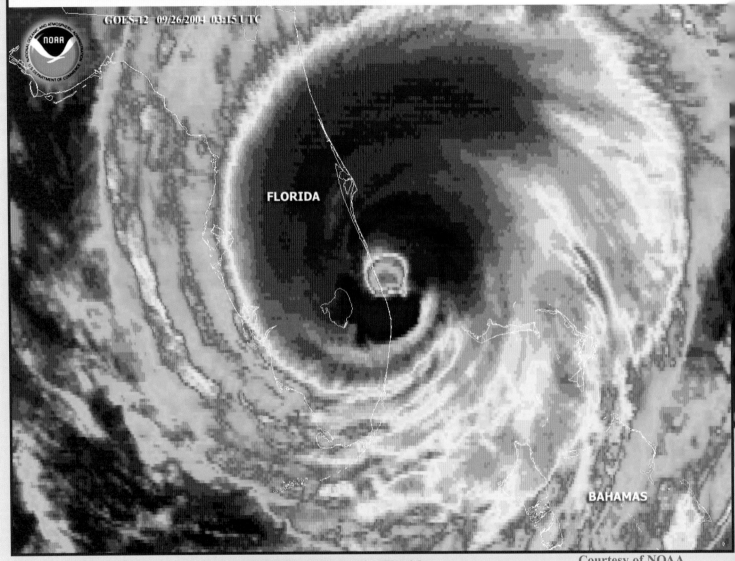

2004 Hurricanes in Florida

Courtesy of NOAA

Name	Date of Landfall	Category	Wind Speed at Landfall	Property Damage
Charley	8/13	4	145 mph	$14 billion
Frances	9/5	2	105 mph	$8.9 billion
Ivan	9/16	3	130 mph	$13 billion
Jeanne	9/26	3	120 mph	$6.5 billion

TOTAL DAMAGE: $42 BILLION +

Charley, Frances, Ivan, and Jeanne

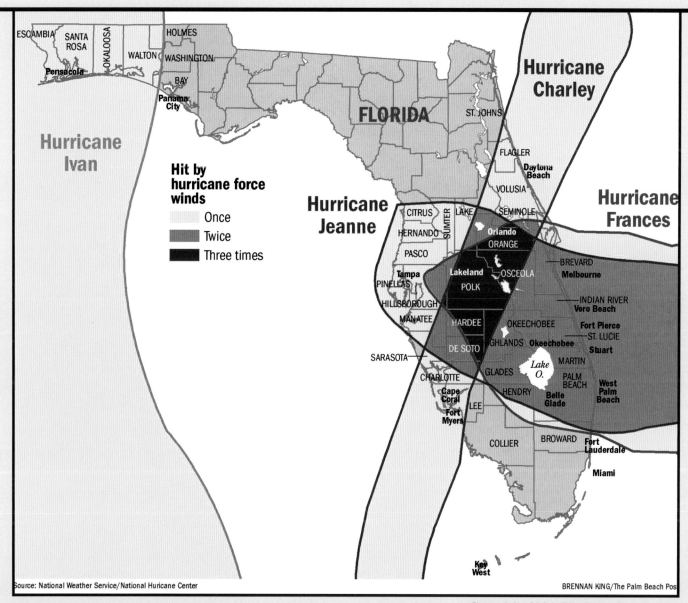

Source: National Weather Service/National Huricane Center

BRENNAN KING/The Palm Beach Pos

This map shows the tracks of all four of our 2004 storms. The area in red was hit by three hurricanes! Although Florida has never had four hurricanes in one year, this increased hurricane activity is typical of the current weather trends. Be prepared for increased hurricane activity until about 2020.

Hurricanes in Last Century:

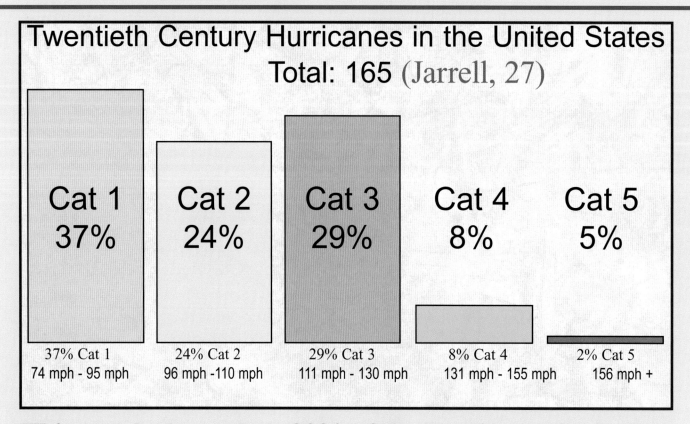

Twentieth Century Hurricanes in the United States
Total: 165 (Jarrell, 27)

Cat 1 37%	Cat 2 24%	Cat 3 29%	Cat 4 8%	Cat 5 5%
37% Cat 1 74 mph - 95 mph	24% Cat 2 96 mph -110 mph	29% Cat 3 111 mph - 130 mph	8% Cat 4 131 mph - 155 mph	2% Cat 5 156 mph +

This graph shows that **90% of the hurricanes in the last century were cat 3's or less.** Since winds from cat 4 and cat 5 storms can devastate any landscape, this book deals with the much more common cat 1 - cat 3 hurricanes, or the winds that are far enough away from the eye of the cat 4's and 5's to avoid total devastation.

Much of the damage done by these storms (cat 1 - cat 3) is to vegetation, with the exception of the poor souls who live or own property very near the eye or are flooded. Roof damage is the second most common damage in these storms.

How strong were they?

Above: Cat 1 through cat 3 storms do the most damage to vegetation and roofs. Photo by Stephen Brown.

Above: Category 5 storms do serious structural damage, as shown in this photograph of a home in south Miami-Dade County after hurricane Andrew. Photo from FEMA.

Hurricanes in Florida:

Above: Houses on Sanibel after Charley. Photo by Randy Isler.

Hurricane forecasters report that the number of hurricanes per year run in cycles. These cycles have been clearly evident for the last century, as shown on the previous pages. They are part of natural weather patterns and tend to last for twenty or more years.

Weather experts reported that 1995 was the beginning of a new cycle of increased hurricane activity that would last for thirty years. Although the years from 1995 to 2000 had more hurricanes than any five years on record, it was the 2004 season that really caught our attention. I moved to Florida in 1974 and experienced my first hurricane in 2004... and my second a few weeks later! Most Floridians had never experienced a Florida hurricane, and within a month millions had experienced one, two, or even three hurricanes.

We have twenty years left of this increased activity. Let's do our best to limit its impact on our landscape.

Current Trends Now Have Our Total Attention.

Above: Pensacola Federation of Garden Clubs' building after Ivan. Photo by Carol Whitmer.

Effect of the proximity to the eye...

Areas close to the eye of a hurricane (particularly to the north) are often completely stripped of vegetation. But these areas are small compared the the entire area that receives hurricane-force winds from the same storm. The focus of this book is to landscape areas in order to minimize wind damage *away from the eye of the storm*. For the unfortunate plants that are unlucky enough to be near the eye, there's not much we can do.

Above: Take a look at ground zero. This spot on Hutchinson Island is near the eye of two hurricanes that made landfall in 2004, both Frances and Jeanne. This photo was taken about two months after the storms. The vegetation is dead, which is typical of areas that are near the eye of any size hurricane.

Compare these three trees just miles apart.

Left: This sabal palm is about a mile south of the devastation shown opposite, about 200 feet from the beach. It is alive and well. The difference between these two photos shows that hurricanes wipe out __all__ of the vegetation in a very small area.

Right: This magnolia tree is a few miles inland from the photo above. Just these few miles make the difference between complete devastation and having the majority of the wind-tolerant plants still alive.

Effect of the strength of the storm..

The difference in the amount of damage between a category 2 storm and a category 5 storm is startling. I drove the coast of Mississippi a few months after Camille, the strongest cat 5 on record. There was nothing but rubble for miles, a full three blocks in from the beach. I didn't see a single wall standing from any building. I also visited ground zero from cat 5 hurricane Andrew many times. Whole neighborhoods were destroyed. What a difference I found when driving Hutchinson Island, victim of a cat 2 and a cat 3 hurricane within a month. Although many buildings were damaged, very few had fallen. Luckily, cat 5 storms are rare.

The effect on vegetation varies greatly between storms of different strengths. If you are near the eye of a cat 4 or cat 5, don't count on seeing too many trees standing after the storm, regardless of their wind tolerance. However, a few miles makes a lot of difference. The majority of areas affected by hurricanes are affected by lower winds that cover much greater areas than the small eyes do. In these huge areas, what you plant and how you plant it makes a lot of difference.

Above: After Andrew, a cat 5 storm, the areas that were hardest hit had very little vegetation left. But remember, only two percent of all hurricanes are this strong. What you plant can make a lot of difference in more common cat 1 to cat 3 storms. Photo from FEMA.

From Cat 1 to Cat 5

In areas hit by hurricane-force winds from these categories of storms, the following historical losses were recorded. Note that these numbers reflect the entire area affected by the hurricane. For example, the numbers for hurricane Andrew reflect the entire area around Andrew with winds of over 74 mph, not just the area of 156 mph winds.

Category 1 (winds 74-95 mph): **Erin, slow-moving 85 mph, 11% of surveyed trees went down (14).**

Category 2 (winds 96-110 mph): **No historical statistics.**

Category 3 (winds 111-130 mph): **Opal, faster moving 125 mph, 13% of surveyed trees went down. This figure would have been higher had not Erin hit the same area a short time earlier (14).**

Category 4 (winds 131-155 mph): **In Hugo, Charleston lost up to 45% of all landscape trees (14).**

Category 5 (winds 156 mph+): **In Andrew, 38% of all the trees died. Almost every tree had more than 50% of the canopy damaged (14).**

Above: Even after cat 4 storms like this site hit by Charley, some vegetation remains standing while others fall. The plant with the huge root ball is an Australian pine, which falls in cat 1 storms. Notice how many wind-tolerant palms are left standing. This homeowner must have paid thousands of dollars to have this one tree removed. I'll be he won't allow any more of these on his property! Photo by Rusty Isler.

Eight Important Hurricane Facts

1. **Storm surge is worse on the west coast of Florida** than the east coast because the water is more shallow off the west coast.

2. **West coast storms move faster** than those on the east coast.

3. **The effects of a faster storm are felt further inland** as exemplified by what happened to Arcadia in hurricane Charley, which moved quickly. Arcadia is about twenty miles inland from Punta Gorda, where the storm made landfall. The damage in Arcadia was massive.

4. **Barrier islands are the most vulnerable locations.**

5. **Palm Beach County's 28 inches of rain** in September 2004, broke all previous records.

6. **Hurricane Camille was the strongest storm to directly strike the US .** We have learned a lot from previous storms, but seem to forget quickly. According to Pielke: "Without fail, in the aftermath of every hurricane's impact, general lessons for coping with hurricanes are drawn, but typically are soon forgotten, and to have be relearned by another community in the aftermath of the next hurricane...One element in motivating proactive action with respect to hurricanes is a solid foundation of knowledge of the lessons of experience" (40).

7. **Winds can change direction numerous times.** This happened in Camille, and is considered partially responsible for the complete destruction of certain areas (40).

8. **Hurricanes are the most costly natural disaster in the United States.**

Left: Flooding causes tremendous plant damage after hurricanes. Many landscape plants can take one day under water, but with more than that, they die. We had four days of standing water in a portion of our garden and lost all the plants in that section of our property. Photo by Daniel Culbert.

Left: Barrier islands are the most vulnerable spots for hurricanes. Photo by Hans Wilson.

Right: Although the wind may have blown from only one direction at your house, it can blow from any direction at any spot in Florida. Be prepared from every angle. Photo by Carol Hall.

Chapter 2

Know your Plant's
Wind Tolerance

Although Florida has had its share of hurricanes, most residents have not had frequent experiences with them. There is often a twenty or thirty year delay between hurricanes hitting the same area. Many areas of Florida have never had a hurricane.

These long delays make people forget from one storm to another what works and what doesn't in the landscape. Since the majority of hurricanes we encounter are "vegetation storms," the damage is more to our landscape than to our structures. Look at the legendary 2004 hurricane season in Florida - we had four hurricanes within about two months. About 100,000 people went through winds over 130 mph. These people lost a lot more than trees - many lost their homes and businesses.

Most of us (about 7,000,000 people), however, who were affected by the 2004 hurricanes experienced winds of 70 to 95 miles per hour. These wind speeds cause a lot more damage to vegetation than to structures. Although neighborhoods are littered with blue tarps on roofs, showing the roof had damage and is awaiting repairs, the devastation to the landscape is worse. Streets are littered with trees so that no one can pass. Trees are piled on top of houses, causing major structural damage.

Left: In the 2004 hurricane season, the ficus trees in south Florida caused more damage than any other species. Why didn't we learn from Andrew in 1991, where Miami had the same problem? Tens of thousands of ficus were planted in Broward and Palm Beach County after hurricane Andrew because they are fast-growing and inexpensive. The poor souls who end up having to pay to have the big ones removed quickly find out it costs about as much as a small car or a large engagement ring. Let's not make the same mistake again.

Some plants tolerate wind...

Above: These trees were all subjected to the same wind. What made one fall and others stand? Different species of trees tolerate wind differently. Photo by Rusty Isler.

In these photos, why are some trees down and others still standing? They were all subjected to the same winds, and although many different factors affect a tree's stability, the most important is the tree's wind tolerance.

Some trees, like ironwoods, have very strong wood and a root system that goes deep into the ground to keep the trees stable. Their canopies are loose enough to let the wind blow through them rather than blowing them over.

Other trees have shallow root systems, weak wood, and dense canopies. These three factors cause trees to fall easier.

much better than others.

Above: Tabebuias fall in winds as low as 25 mph. They are one of the weakest trees commonly planted in south Florida.

Above, left: Hong Kong orchid trees fall easily because they have dense canopies and brittle wood. Right: Australian pines fall easily because they have shallow roots. Photo by Rusty Isler.

Know your Plant's Wind Tolerance.

Sometimes there is nothing you can do. If you get a direct hit from a cat 5, it doesn't matter what you plant because no plant can stand up to 160 mph winds. But remember that 90% of storms are cat 3 and below, and many trees will survive those winds, particularly if you are away from the eye.

It's time for intelligent planting. Know the wind tolerance of every plant you buy. And stick to wind-tolerant trees for the areas that could fall on your house.

Look at these three photos of plants in the same garden, about twenty miles south of the eye of Frances (cat 2) and Jeanne (cat 3). Some were destroyed, and some look like nothing happened. This difference in damage is primarily due to differences in the plants' ability to withstand wind.

By using this book with its companions, "Easy Gardens for Florida" and "Best Garden Color for Florida", you can find out the wind tolerance of most commonly used landscape plants, and a lot of more unique ones as well.

Above: The entire top of this ylang ylang tree snapped off. This doesn't mean that no one should ever plant a ylang ylang again - it is one of the best trees for scent in the tropics. But know ahead of time that it might break in the next storm and place it so that it will do minimal damage.

Opposite, above: A pygmy date palm in the same garden shows no signs of damage at all. This is one of the most wind-tolerant palms available, even surviving well from hurricane Andrew (cat 5).

Opposite, below: These crotons also look untouched because they are very wind-tolerant. They did not even need cutting back after the storms.

On the whole, palms tolerate wind...

This photo presents a familiar scene to many Floridians who have weathered storms - the shade tree is knocked down, but the palms stand tall. Photo by Stephen Brown.

An area near the spot where Charley made landfall, just outside Punta Gorda near the Peace River. Notice how the the oak died but the sabal palm is standing tall. This photo was taken about three months after the storm. Oaks that were just a little bit further away from the eye had started leafing out by this time. Photo by Barbara Hadsell.

This photo was taken on Bokeelia shortly after Charley. Although the royal palms look like they are in bad shape, most of them are starting to recover. Photo by Stephen Brown.

better than shade trees.

Sabal palms in Punta Gorda shortly after Charley. They stood tall while buildings around them crumbled. The sabal palm is the second-most wind-tolerant tree in Florida. Photo by Allan Theisen.

The pygmy date palm is the strongest palm we have. It even stood tall in hurricane Andrew (cat 5). Look at how perfect this palm looks compared with the building behind it! Photo by Rusty Isler.

This photo was taken by Daniel Culbert shortly after Charley devastated this town, Arcadia. These are Canary Island date palms and are relatives of the pygmy date palms shown above. They are incredibly strong.

But not all palms are wind-tolerant...

Above; Queen palm down from Charley. Photo by Stephen Brown.

Left: Queen palms are one of the most common palms used in south and central Florida. They have very little tolerance for wind, as shown at this site in Punta Gorda. Photo by Allan Theisen.

Queen palms fall easily.

Above: Carol Hall's queen palm fell at her home in Palm Beach Gardens, about twenty miles southwest of the eyes of Frances and Jeanne. Photo by Carol Hall.

Right: Many queen palms that did not go down completely just bent to the point of being dangerous, like this one in Stuart.

Do native trees hold up better than exotics?

Above: Laurel Oaks that fell as a result of hurricane Ivan. Dan Mullen took the photo. Although this is not his house, he had 15 laurel oaks fall on his nearby property.

Native trees were present in Florida before Christopher Columbus discovered America. Exotics are trees that have been introduced into Florida after 1492. Native trees held up better than exotic trees in south Florida. Dr. Mary Duryea found that native trees fared better than exotics in south Florida after hurricane Andrew: "Native tree species...were the best survivors in the wind...34% of the exotic trees were still standing after the hurricane (Andrew) while 66% of native trees were standing"(13).

However, the jury is still out about whether the natives did better than exotics in central and north Florida. Water oaks and laurel oaks, both natives, were two of the worst trees in these areas during the four storms of 2004.

Many exotics show amazing wind tolerance, like the date palms shown on the opposite page that were photographed at the Breakers Hotel in Palm Beach just a few weeks after it had been hit by two hurricanes! Some exotics are from areas of the world that are quite windy and are well-adapted to it. To be on the safe side, check out the tree's wind tolerance before assuming that all native trees stand up beautifully in hurricanes.

24 Great trees for our windy times.

Bald Cypress (Zones 4-11, grow in sun) is a very tall tree that is not only wind tolerant but also water tolerant. It grows throughout Florida. This versatility makes it useful in areas that may flood in hurricanes. It is bare in the winter, however. See more about this tree on page 67.

Crepe Myrtle (Zones 7-10b, grow in sun.) offers great wind resistance and flowers in summer. It grows to about 20 feet, and thrives in most of the state. Crepe myrtles are bare in winter. See the reports from around the state on page 66.

Dogwood (Zones 7-9a, grow in light to medium shade) is a traditional tree for central and north Florida which offers pink or white flowers and excellent wind tolerance. It reaches 20 to 30 feet in height. See page 68 for news from around the state. Photos by Doug Caldwell.

Gumbo Limbo (Zones 9b-11, grow in sun.) loses a lot of branches but stands up well to at least cat 3 winds and takes flooding better than most trees. It reaches 40 feet in height and is partially bare in winter. Read more on page 71.

Ironwood (Zones 9b-11, grow in sun to light shade.) is a little-known tree that showed amazing wind resistance in the few examples we have. It slowly grows to about 20 feet tall and drops berries. Read more on page 72. Photo by Joan Brookwell.

Japanese Maple (Zones 5-9a, grow in light to medium shade) is a good choice for the northern half of the state for wind tolerance. It is a small, slow-growing tree, eventually reaching 20 feet in height. Read more on page 76. Photo by Daniel Culbert and includes his mother!

Lignum Vitae (Zones 10-11, grow in sun to light shade) is a lovely, small, slow-growing tree that is native to south Florida and thrives there. It eventually grows to 20 feet in height. Great wind resistance. Read more on page 74. Photo by Gene Joyner.

Live Oak (Zones 5 -11, grow in sun to light shade) is a large tree that has consistently been categorized as the most wind-tolerant shade tree for the entire state of Florida. It can be too large for many houses, however. Consider a sand live oak if you need something smaller. Read more on page 78.

Magnolia, Southern (Zones 7-10b, grow in sun) is a traditional southern tree that really performed well in the last four hurricanes. Although it grows 75 feet tall, the "Little Gem" magnolia is much smaller, and quite wind tolerant as well. Read more on page 74 about the southern magnolia.

Palm, Canary Island Date (Zones 9a-11, grow in sun) is a stately, large palm that has problems with some pests and diseases but holds up great in high winds. It is quite expensive. Read more on page 79.

Palm, Date (Zones 9b-11, grow in sun) *Phoenix dactilyfera* is related to the Canary Island date palm and has many of the same characteristics. Read more on page 80.

Palm, Foxtail (Zones 10-11, grow in sun to light shade) is a relatively new palm for south Florida that did quite well during the storms of 2004. It grows to about 30 feet tall. Read more on page 81.

24 Great trees for our windy times.

Palm, Pindo (Zones 8-10b, grow in sun) is used primarily in central and north Florida. It didn't do as well as the date palms but is one of the better palms for colder areas. Read more on page 81.

Palm, Pygmy Date (Zones 9-11, grow in sun or medium shade) is the number one tree for wind tolerance in south and central Florida. It grows slowly to a height of about 10 feet tall and comes with either one or multiple trunks. Read more on page 81.

Palm, Royal (Zones 10-11, grow in sun) is a Florida native that offers good wind resistance in storms up to cat 4. This is a very tall palm, growing to 60 feet. Foxtail palms have the same look without the extreme height. Read more on page 82.

Sabal Palm (Zones 8-11, grow in sun to light shade) is one of our most amazing native trees, some reaching 30 feet. It is number two in wind tolerance, following the number one pygmy date palm. Read more on page 82.

Palm, Saw Palmetto (Zones 8-11, grow in sun to light shade) is another tough-as-nails native that thrives in high winds. Although it grows slowly, it makes a great wind screen because it grows in a cluster. Read more on page 82.

Palm, Thatch (Zones 10-11, grow in sun to medium shade) is a native palm that tolerates a lot of wind. This palm should be used much more in south Florida. It's small size, 20 feet tall, makes it particularly useful. Read more on page 83.

Red Bay (Zones 8-11, grow in sun to light shade) is a good tree for wind tolerance in any part of Florida. It reaches 40 feet in height and is occasionally bothered by disfiguring galls caused by an insect. Read more on page 85. Photo by Gene Joyner.

Sand Live Oak (Zones 8 -11j, grow in sun to light shade) is a smaller version (20 to 30 feet tall) of the live oak that could be quite useful, especially where wind tolerance is needed along with a smaller size. It stains driveways. Read more on page 78. Photo by Joan Brookwell.

Seagrape (Zones 9b-11, grow in sun) is another strong native, provided it is allowed to grow in its natural, multi-trunked form. This tree grows to 30 feet and drops a lot of leaves. Read more on page 86.

Stopper, Redberry (Zones 10-11, grow in sun to medium shade) is a small tree for south Florida that grows to 20 feet and holds up very well in wind. This size is quite useful for residences. Read more on page 87.

Stopper, Spanish (Zones 9b-11, grow in sun to light shade) is used as a tree or a tall, narrow shrub that did extremely well in the 2004 hurricanes. It grows slowly to a height of 20 feet in south and south-central Florida. Read more on page 87.

Stopper, White (Zones 8-11, grow in sun to medium shade.) Strong shrub or small tree that smells like a skunk and grows throughout Florida. It grows with a narrow form to 20 feet tall and takes a lot of shade. Read more on page 87.

Lessons from the Three Worst Trees

Australian pines are one of the worst trees to have anywhere near you in a hurricane. They not only fall easily, but the root ball comes out of the ground, leaving you with a mass that weighs tons and often costs thousands of dollars for disposal.

Australian pines grow primarily in the southern part of the state in frost-free areas. But with the current warming trend, their range is expanding towards the north.

These are invasive trees meaning they disrupt our natural ecosystems, crowding out our native plants, which is all the more reason to have them removed.

One fell in my nursery, taking five native trees with it. It not only cost $3500 to remove the mess, but it crushed about twenty percent of my nursery plants!

I recommend that you remove any of these trees within falling distance of any structure. It would be best do it before the next storm season. There are a lot of great trees to use as replacements.

Above: A clump of Australian pines just waiting to fall down during the next hurricane.
Opposite, above: The root ball of the Australian pine that fell in my nursery. It cost a fortune to remove.
Opposite, below: One Australian pine fell in my nursery. It took five other native trees with it. The mass was so large that it crushed about twenty percent of my nursery plants.

1. Australian Pines

Lessons from the Three Worst Trees

Photos above and opposite top: Rusty Isler   *Photo opposite bottom: Stephen Brown*

These photos were taken on Sanibel and Captiva shortly after Charley. If you have any of these within falling distance of your house, have them removed. They fall in 70 mph winds and are quite a danger in south Florida.

According to Dr. Robert Loflin, the Natural Resources Director of Sanibel, it cost $6,000,000 to haul and burn the trash from Charley. Sixty percent ($3,600,000) was one kind of tree, this one! Sanibel and Captiva have 6,500 permanent residents, so it costs $553 per resident just to haul and burn the fallen Australian pines! This number does not include the price the property owner paid to get these monsters cut up and hauled to the street!

According to Dr. Mary Duryea, 96% of these trees fell in hurricane Andrew (14). Millions of these trees are still left standing, throughout south Florida.

1. Australian Pines

Lessons from the Three Worst Trees

We knew about ficus trees before the 2004 hurricanes. In 1991, after hurricane Andrew, we learned that ficus not only blew over easily but also cost a fortune to remove. We kept planting them by the thousands!

The ficus tree on the opposite page would cost about $10,000 to remove. And that doesn't include replacing the building it crushed on the way down. That's as much as a small car or a big engagement ring! And, it's not even covered by insurance!

One golf club in Palm Beach County spent $160,000 just removing these trees, to say nothing of repairing the damage done to whatever was underneath.

It's time for intelligent planting. Know the wind tolerance of every plant you buy. And stick to wind-tolerant trees for locations where they could fall on your house.

Other species of Ficus, like the *Ficus aurea* or strangler fig, do better in hurricanes. The *Ficus altissima* is slightly better, particularly if you let the aerial roots grow so they anchor the tree better.

If you have a *Ficus benjamina* within falling distance of a structure, remove it before it removes you during the next hurricane.

2. Ficus benjamina

Lessons from the Three Worst Trees

Above and opposite: Scenes of laurel oaks. These photos were taken shortly after Ivan in the panhandle by Dan Mullins shortly after Ivan. He had 15 laurel oaks down in his yard!

We had more reports of laurel oaks down than any other tree in central and north Florida. If you have one of these within falling distance of your house, remove it, especially if it is an older tree. Laurel oaks are weaker and shorter lived than live oaks, and the four storms of 2004 proved that the older ones were particularly dangerous.

Officials from Santa Rosa County which was badly hit by Ivan, estimated that 50% of the tree debris was from laurel oaks and water oaks. Imagine that! All that destruction from just two kinds of trees!

3. Laurel Oak

Lessons from the Three Worst Trees

John Atkin's grandfather planted this tree in 1952 at their home in Jay, Florida - about 30 miles from the landfall of hurricane Ivan. Little did he know that this tree would destroy the house 52 years later!

John, his wife Lynn, and their four children - David, Adam, J.D., and Sydney - lived in the house at the time. Luckily, John had a premonition that they should leave the house before the storm, so they spent the time during Ivan with friends.

The tree hit the roof in such a way that it caused a huge split, through which rain water entered. The house was ruined - it could not be repaired.

John and his family moved in with relatives, four of them sharing one room. A few months later, FEMA came up with a camper for the older boy. Later, John and Lynn were able to find a single-wide trailer to live in with their family until the old house could be torn down and a new one built. Contractors are busy in the panhandle, and it could be a year or two more until the new house is built.

All this - three years of stress, financial loss, and family upheaval - because of one tree! If you have wind-sensitive trees planted within falling distance of your home, have the good sense to remove them before the next hurricane.

3. Laurel Oak

These photos show some of the worst trees in Florida for wind tolerance. There are many more that I would not want near my house. See the last section of this chapter, "Wind Tolerance of Florida Plants: Information from around the State," to find more weak plants as well as more information about these. Photos: cherry laurel, redbud, and whole water oak, Joan Brookwell; drake elm, Leon Koneiczny; laurel oak, sand pine, and close-up of water oak, Gene Joyner; tabebuia, Rusty Isler.

Acacia, Ear Leaf

Australian Pine

Cherry Laurel

Drake Elm

Ficus benjamina

Laurel Oak

Queen Palm

Redbud

Sand Pine

Tabebuia

Water Oak

Florida Gardening Series, Volume 1
EASY GARDENS for SOUTH FLORIDA

• companion to Best Garden Color for Florida
• simple landscape plants and gardens
by Pamela Crawford

Florida Gardening Series Volume 2
Best Garden Color for Florida

• primarily for USDA Zones 9 through 11 in Florida
• best annuals, perennials, flowering shrubs, & trees
• companion to "Easy Gardens for Florida"
by Pamela Crawford

Botanical Name: *Quercus virginiana*

Common Name: **Live Oak**

CHARACTERISTICS

PLANT TYPE: Large tree

AVERAGE SIZE: 40 to 50 feet tall by 50 to 60 feet wide.

GROWTH RATE: Medium; grows faster with supplemental water and fertilizer.

LEAF: Dark olive green with a gray cast; about 2 inches long by 1/2 inch wide. Leaves on the new growth have smooth sides. Older leaves show some serrations along the sides. Laurel Oak leaves have smooth sides on all leaves.

FLOWER: Inconspicuous

BEST COLOR: No seasonal variation, except the tree is partially deciduous (fewer leaves in the winter).

AVERAGE LIFE: 100 years

ORIGIN: Southeastern U.S., Central America, Cuba, and Mexico.

CAUTIONS: Partially deciduous, as it is not as full in the winter, but never completely without leaves. Also, damages pavement if planted too close.

SPACING: 30 to 40 feet on center.

One of the best trees in south Florida for attracting wildlife. Easy and beautiful.

The best features of the Live Oak are its spreading canopy and rough bark. Notice how much sunlight shines through the branches.

General: Live Oaks are the most beautiful shade trees in south Florida. Their beauty lies in the spreading, graceful structure of the branches and the rough bark. Many other plants, like Orchids, Resurrection Fern, and Spanish Moss, attach themselves to the trunk, anchored by this rough bark. Mature Live Oaks sometimes look like entire ecosystems, with gardens of natural plants supported by their branches. Many of our south Florida shade trees produce shade too dense for underplantings, and the area underneath becomes sand. Not so for Live Oaks. Their dappled shade is ideal for many of south Florida's lushest foliage. The tree is partially deciduous, not as full in winter as summer. And, it is not particularly attractive when young. But a little patience produces a great reward - a mature Live Oak.

180   EASY GARDENS FOR SOUTH FLORIDA

Both of this book's companions ("Easy Gardens for Florida" and "Best Garden Color for Florida") include hundreds of plant profiles (example above) of great plants for the Florida landscape. Each profile includes wind tolerance of the plant, along with the other valuable information you need to know. You need to know a lot more about a plant than just its wind tolerance before buying it. Find that information in these two books.

to learn about a plant's wind-tolerance.

Companions: For a woodland garden, plant masses of Fishtail Ferns and Wart Ferns under an Oak. Add color accents, like Starburst Pentas, Blue Porterflower, Yellow Mussaenda, Walking Iris, Dwarf Powderpuff, and Shrimp. The dappled shade under a Live Oak is ideal for this plant material.

The lower branches of the large Live Oak have been trimmed to show the house. The medium Live Oak is too small to trim in this fashion.

Care in the Landscape: Live Oaks require little care. They form naturally into good specimens without a lot of pruning. Remove crossed branches and dead wood every few years. Live Oaks do not require fertilizer in average Florida soils. But, if faster growth is desired, fertilize in March, June, and October with a well-balanced, slow-release mix with minor elements. Supplemental water also increases the growth rate of these trees. Live Oaks drop leaves all year. Raking can be a nuisance if grass is planted underneath or the leaves fall on pavement. Oak leaves are one of the best mulches available for the garden.

GROWING CONDITIONS

LIGHT: Light shade to full sun.

WATER: Low, but tolerates irrigation up to 3 times per week. Lives without irrigation in many parts of south Florida after its initial establishment period. Oaks often defoliate after being transplanted, but leaves reappear quickly.

SOIL: Wide range

SALT TOLERANCE: High

WIND TOLERANCE: High

ZONE: 5 to 11. Survives temperatures well below freezing.

PEST PROBLEMS: Galls, root rot.

PROPAGATION: Seeds

Note: The spreading character of the Live Oak is well shown on pages 300 and 301.

LARGE TREES 181

Take these books with you when you shop for plants so that you can have all the information you need at your finger tips. It is much better to know the good and the bad about a plant before you plant it in your garden.

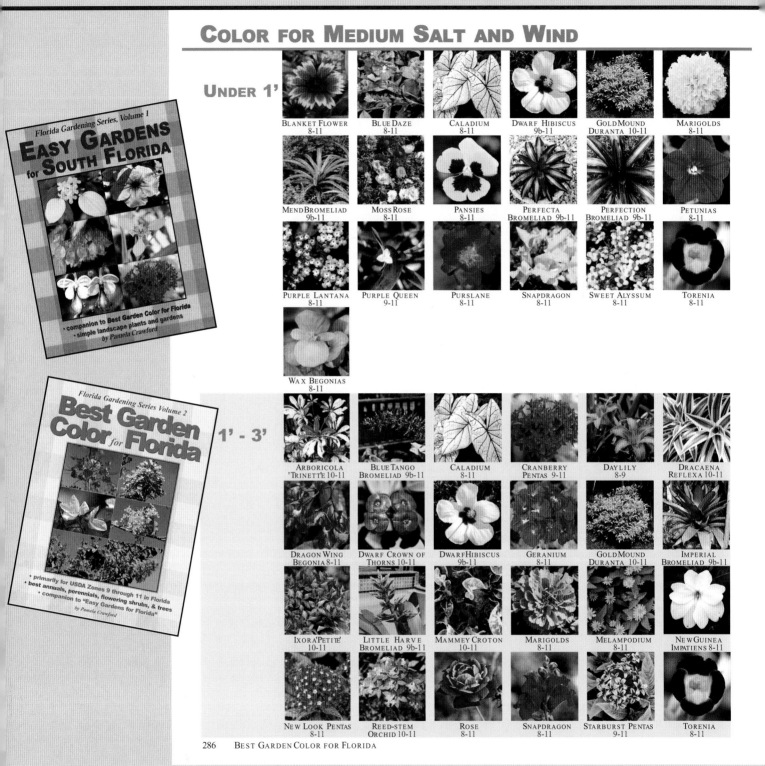

COLOR FOR MEDIUM SALT AND WIND

UNDER 1'

BLANKET FLOWER 8-11	BLUE DAZE 8-11	CALADIUM 8-11	DWARF HIBISCUS 9b-11	GOLD MOUND DURANTA 10-11	MARIGOLDS 8-11
MEND BROMELIAD 9b-11	MOSS ROSE 8-11	PANSIES 8-11	PERFECTA BROMELIAD 9b-11	PERFECTION BROMELIAD 9b-11	PETUNIAS 8-11
PURPLE LANTANA 8-11	PURPLE QUEEN 9-11	PURSLANE 8-11	SNAPDRAGON 8-11	SWEET ALYSSUM 8-11	TORENIA 8-11
WAX BEGONIAS 8-11					

1' - 3'

ARBORICOLA 'TRINETTE' 10-11	BLUE TANGO BROMELIAD 9b-11	CALADIUM 8-11	CRANBERRY PENTAS 9-11	DAY LILY 8-9	DRACAENA REFLEXA 10-11
DRAGON WING BEGONIA 8-11	DWARF CROWN OF THORNS 10-11	DWARF HIBISCUS 9b-11	GERANIUM 8-11	GOLD MOUND DURANTA 10-11	IMPERIAL BROMELIAD 9b-11
IXORA 'PETITE' 10-11	LITTLE HARVE BROMELIAD 9b-11	MAMMEY CROTON 10-11	MARIGOLDS 8-11	MELAMPODIUM 8-11	NEW GUINEA IMPATIENS 8-11
NEW LOOK PENTAS 8-11	REED-STEM ORCHID 10-11	ROSE 8-11	SNAPDRAGON 8-11	STARBURST PENTAS 9-11	TORENIA 8-11

286   BEST GARDEN COLOR FOR FLORIDA

Florida Gardening Series, Volume 1
EASY GARDENS for SOUTH FLORIDA
• companion to Best Garden Color for Florida
• simple landscape plants and gardens
by Pamela Crawford

Florida Gardening Series Volume 2
Best Garden Color for Florida
• primarily for USDA Zones 9 through 11 in Florida
• best annuals, perennials, flowering shrubs, & trees
• companion to "Easy Gardens for Florida"
by Pamela Crawford

Both of this book's companions ("Easy Gardens for Florida" and "Best Garden Color for Florida") include photo charts in their chapters on salt and wind. These photo charts show all the plants that are medium or high wind tolerance, organized by size. They are very convenient, because they allow you to look at all of your choices at once, like a list with photos!

to learn about a plant's wind-tolerance.

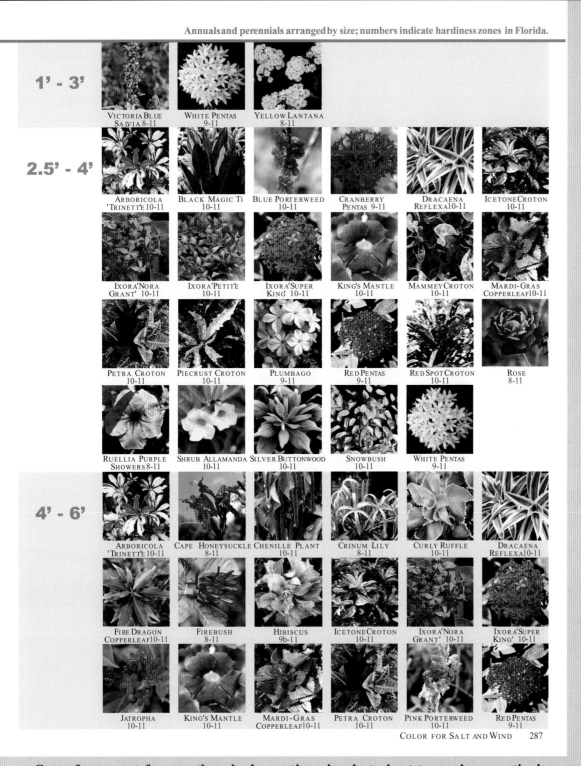

Annuals and perennials arranged by size; numbers indicate hardiness zones in Florida.

1' - 3'

VICTORIA BLUE SALVIA 8-11 | WHITE PENTAS 9-11 | YELLOW LANTANA 8-11

2.5' - 4'

ARBORICOLA 'TRINETTE' 10-11 | BLACK MAGIC TI 10-11 | BLUE PORTERWEED 10-11 | CRANBERRY PENTAS 9-11 | DRACAENA REFLEXA 10-11 | ICETONE CROTON 10-11

IXORA 'NORA GRANT' 10-11 | IXORA 'PETITE' 10-11 | IXORA 'SUPER KING' 10-11 | KING'S MANTLE 10-11 | MAMMEY CROTON 10-11 | MARDI-GRAS COPPERLEAF 10-11

PETRA CROTON 10-11 | PIECRUST CROTON 10-11 | PLUMBAGO 9-11 | RED PENTAS 9-11 | RED SPOT CROTON 10-11 | ROSE 8-11

RUELLIA PURPLE SHOWERS 8-11 | SHRUB ALLAMANDA 10-11 | SILVER BUTTONWOOD 10-11 | SNOWBUSH 10-11 | WHITE PENTAS 9-11

4' - 6'

ARBORICOLA 'TRINETTE' 10-11 | CAPE HONEYSUCKLE 8-11 | CHENILLE PLANT 10-11 | CRINUM LILY 8-11 | CURLY RUFFLE 10-11 | DRACAENA REFLEXA 10-11

FIRE DRAGON COPPERLEAF 10-11 | FIREBUSH 8-11 | HIBISCUS 9b-11 | ICETONE CROTON 10-11 | IXORA 'NORA GRANT' 10-11 | IXORA 'SUPER KING' 10-11

JATROPHA 10-11 | KING'S MANTLE 10-11 | MARDI-GRAS COPPERLEAF 10-11 | PETRA CROTON 10-11 | PINK PORTERWEED 10-11 | RED PENTAS 9-11

COLOR FOR SALT AND WIND   287

One of my most frequently asked questions is what plant to use in a particular spot. In order to make that decision, you first need to know all the possibilities. These photo charts make that process easy. I have become addicted to them and use them constantly when deciding what to put in a particular spot in my gardens.

Wind-Tolerance of Florida Plants

After the four Florida hurricanes of 2004, I realized that, for first time, we had a lot of available data on plant's wind tolerance. Had I been able to hire about a thousand scientists, I would have had them traveling around Florida counting trees and using scientific methods to give us definitive information on every plant species that grows inside our borders. However, since I just had Barbara Hadsell and myself to do the research, we contacted experts and homeowners alike to gather any and all information we could find to share with you.

We had a great response to our inquiries, particularly from county extension agents in the areas that were hurt the worst by the 2004 storms.

Most of this information is not scientific but anecdotal, meaning information that is passed from person to person mostly by word of mouth or email. And I did not start out with a list of great plants to write about: rather, I accepted what I had observed, could read, or heard about from other people. Although it's not perfect, it's a start. I look forward to this book evolving through the years as more people share information with me about their observations of a plant's wind tolerance.

You will learn in the next chapter about fifteen factors - other than a tree's wind tolerance - that cause them to fall in winds. These factors, such as wet soil, make it even more difficult to judge anecdotal evidence. For example, I had a call from a lady in Lake Worth (80 mph winds) who told me her live oak tree had fallen. Since the live oak is one of our strongest trees, it is quite unusual for one to fall in such low winds. After investigating further, I discovered that her tree was planted within a few feet of her driveway. Since the roots of the tree resisted growing under concrete, her tree had lost the stability on that side and fell over. Another friend sent me photos of her live oak down in Loxahatchee (80 mph winds). It had fallen apart, which again is very unusual for that type of tree in those winds. After investigating further, I found out it was a water oak, which is one of the least wind-tolerant trees in Florida! So, you quicky learn that judging a tree's wind tolerance can be quite tricky. And there are <u>bound</u> to be errors. But, I feel strongly that some information is much better than none at all.

I attempted to put accurate wind speeds with each source. First, I went to the National Hurricane Center and looked at their data. It didn't seem quite right. For example, they estimated the wind at my house at 50 mph, but I had hundreds of trees down. Most of the houses on my street had severe roof damage, which didn't seem possible for 50 mph winds. So I questioned many other experts and individuals with devices that measure wind. When in doubt, I underestimated the wind speed for safety's sake. I would rather tell someone that a tree went down in 80 mph winds and find out later that the winds were 95 mph rather than have it the other way around.

There are some tree surveys that I referenced that I should mention. Dr. Mary Duryea (Assistant Dean for Research and Assistant Director, IFAS, University of Florida) conducts surveys after all the hurricanes that have hit Florida; she has done that since the mid-80's, including Opal, Erin, and Andrew. This data is valuable because she was able to actually count trees and use scientific methods to determine how they did. Currently, she is analyzing her data from the four storms of 2004, which I look forward to reading upon its completion.

Dr. Duryea has summarized some interesting facts in her surveys. She found that native trees fared better than exotics in south Florida after Hurricane Andrew: "Native tree species...were the best survivors in the wind...34% of the exotic trees were still standing after the hurricane (Andrew) while 66% of native trees were standing."(13) She also has interesting information about how trees fared in the same storm: "In general, fruit trees were severely damaged. Black olive, gumbo limbo, and live oak that were pruned survived better than unpruned trees. Only 18% of all the trees that fell caused property damage."(13)

I don't know if native trees did better in central and north Florida, since they had such extensive damage from two native trees, laurel oaks and water oaks.

Brevard County also conducted a tree survey after Frances and Jeanne, which includes good information.

I am not repeating the wind tolerance of all the plants featured in my other books - simply giving new information.

Information From Throughout the State

There is also wind tolerance information on over two hundred plants in "Easy Gardens for Florida" and "Best Garden Color for Florida." The plant profiles in these books also include much of the other information you need to know before buying a plant.

I received valuable data from the Palm Beach County Chapter of the Florida Native Plant Society. They state the following about their information:

> "The survey was conducted informally within the membership of the Palm Beach Chapter. The main purpose of the survey was to help lead a discussion at our October 2004 meeting. We collected around 40 surveys. This was not a thorough data collection effort and should not be considered as such. Also, information was not collected on non-native plants for comparison.
>
> In general, our survey revealed that native plants fared quite well through the two hurricanes. Our native palms probably came out as the most resilient. Some of our faster growing tropical trees did exactly what they are designed to do - shed limbs (large and small ones). It was interesting to see how the same species of trees did in wet conditions versus high and dry conditions (this was discovered through discussion, not the survey). We also discussed the fate of natives in natural areas versus standing alone in a landscaped front yard. Another point brought about by the survey and then carried on through the discussion is that we really need to "wait and see" how our landscape material will do. While many shrubs seemed stripped of leaves, months later they will return to their glory."

Remember that hurricanes are notoriously unpredictable. Tornadoes and higher wind currents are often reported within these storms, which causes trees to fall when theoretically, they should remain standing. Regardless of how thoroughly we study these storms, there are always surprises. And since so much of this data is anecdotal, that leaves considerable room for error. So use this information as guidelines to help you make intelligent choices.

The numbers with each source correspond to more source information in the "Sources and Bibliography" at the end of this book.

I have classified wind tolerance as follows:

Very high wind tolerance: Plants that hold together fairly well in cat 1 to cat 4 hurricanes; some of the plants in this category, like the pygmy date palm, do fairly well in cat 5 storms as well. I put very few plants in this class of very high wind tolerance, probably underestimating the strength of some plants in dealing with these high winds. I felt it best to err on the side of caution with a study as anecdotal as this one.

High wind tolerance: Plants that hold together pretty well in hurricanes from cat 1 to cat 3 hurricanes. They may not die in stronger hurricanes, but will be pretty torn up.

Medium wind tolerance: Plants that hold together fairly well in cat 1 and cat 2 storms. They may not die in stronger hurricanes, but will be pretty torn up.

Low wind tolerance: Plants that routinely show damage in cat 1 storms. They may not die in stronger hurricanes, but will be pretty torn up. Not all of them show damage, but a significant percentage does show the consequences of the wind.

Acacia, Ear Leaf *(Acacia auriculiformis):* Zones 10 to 11.

This tree is an invasive, exotic tree (meaning that it crowds out our native forests). No one is currently planting it, but a lot of them exist in the landscape, particularly because it reproduces like crazy. It is very brittle, with limbs falling from winds of only about 30 mph. If you have any, consider removing them. **Low wind tolerance.**

Acacia, Sweet *(Acacia farnesiana)* Zones 8b to 11. The Palm Beach Chapter of the Florida Native Plant Society had three reports on this tree's performance during Frances and Jeanne; two of them were 'good' and one of them' 'ok'. However, they did conclude that the tree did well considering. The winds in this county ranged from about 50 to 100 mph during these two storms (19). **Medium wind tolerance** is a guestimate for this tree because I don't have enough data to make an accurate judgement. Since it is a native with an open canopy, it

could possess **high wind tolerance.** More data is needed to know for sure.

African Tulip Tree *(Spathodea campanulata)* Zones 9b to 11.
This tree is brittle, and not recommended for planting within falling distance of buildings. I have one that I planted in the middle of a clump of slash pines. It made it well through Frances and Jeanne, probably because it was protected by the pines. I'm not sure of the winds, but they were at least 80 mph. Had the tree been by itself or had the winds been much stronger, it probably would have fallen or broken up. See "Best Garden Color for Florida" for more information about this tree. Because of its brittleness, this tree has a **low wind tolerance**.

Allamanda (shrub) *(Allamanda schottii):* Zones 10 to 11.

Don Wacker, who lives on a barrier island off Vero Beach and experienced some of the worst winds from Frances

(cat 2) and Jeanne (cat 3) reports that his allamanda "fared well but were close to the foundation of the house on the west side, so they were more protected from wind, even though the back side of the storms hit them directly." (50). See "Easy Gardens for Florida" for more information about this plant. Because of this limited information, I would class this plant as having a **medium wind tolerance**.

Anise *(Illicium floridanum):* Zones 6b to 10a. Beth Bolles of Escambia County (which was ravaged by Ivan) reports that many anise were blown over (2). I am unable to classify this plant with only one report; there is just not enough information available. If you have any information on this one and would like to share it, email me at colorgdn@aol.com.

Arboricola *(Schefflera arboricola):* Zones 10 to 11.

This plant has always been known for its wind tolerance. It even took the 120 mph winds at Don Wacker's house near Vero Beach in stride (50). See more about this plant in "Easy Gardens for Florida" and "Container Gardens for Florida." I'm rating this one as having a **high wind tolerance**. It could have a **very high wind tolerance**, but I don't have enough data about its performance in cat 4 and cat 5 storms.

Information From Throughout the State

Arborvitae *(Thuja occidentalis):*

Holly Shackelford of the Charlotte County Extension reported these plants after the hurricane as "damaged, leaning, with natural form distorted". But they had just been through cat 4 Charley (47). Dan Culbert (11) took a photo of arborvitae (above) that shows its appearance after Frances and Jeanne in Ft. Pierce. It remained standing while the house in the background fell down! This plant has a **high wind tolerance**, but as you can see, it will take it some time for it to recover aesthetically.

Avocado *(Persea americana):* Zones 10 to 11. According to Dr. Mary Duryea's survey after hurricane Andrew (145 mph), 46% were left standing (15). This is a brittle tree, but many more were left standing after the less intense hurricanes, Frances and Jeanne; even though they broke up a lot in these cat 2 and 3 storms, they generally recovered. I wouldn't plant one too near the house, though. Because of its brittleness, avocados have a **low wind tolerance**.

Baby Sun Rose *(Aptenia cordifolia):* Zones 9 to 11.

This is an extremely wind-tolerant ground cover that doesn't have too much color but works well in difficult situations. The photo (above) was taken four weeks after hurricane Jeanne hit at the Breakers Resort at Palm Beach, where the winds hit somewhere around 120 mph. These plants are in containers near the beach and have a **high wind tolerance**.

Beautyberry *(Callicarpa americana):* Zones 8 to 11.

The Palm Beach Chapter of the Florida Native Plant Society had fifteen 'good', five 'ok', and two 'so-so' reports on this shrub's performance during Frances and Jeanne. All agreed that it had done quite well overall. The winds in this county ranged from about 50 to 100 mph during these two storms (19). I have hundreds of them in my woods, and mine did very well in the same county. This plant has either a **medium** or **high wind tolerance**. I need more data about its performance in higher winds.

Begonias, White Odorata *(Begonia odorata alba):* Zones 9b to 11.

We have hundreds of these in our trial gardens and had trimmed them shortly before Frances and Jeanne, so they went into the storms at the height of about two feet tall. They did much better in our 80 mph winds than the taller pink angelwings. I don't know if that is because they are more wind tolerant, or if their low stature helped preserve them. Hurricanes hurt taller plants more than those that are very close to the ground. As look out my window three months after the storms, I notice they are flowering their heads off and looking like no storm hit them. Our nursery crop, however, did not do well. It was under water for four days and had to be discarded. This begonia has a **medium wind tolerance**. For more information about this wonderful plant, see "Best Garden Color for Florida."

Wind-Tolerance of Florida Plants

Begonias, Pink Angelwing
(*Begonia 'Flamingo'*): Zones 9b to 11.

These beautiful plants do not like wind. Most of the taller ones in fairly open areas of our trial gardens were damaged in 80 mph winds beyond the point of no return; we removed them about a month after the storms. The ones planted in very protected areas did all right, like the ones just inside a fence pictured above. I heard from areas where there was more wind than mine that these begonias had lost all their leaves, but were recovering. These begonias also do not like flooding. All the ones in low spots and underwater for four days did not survive. Since this plant blooms all the time, I will continue to plant it and take my chances! For more information about this plant, see both "Easy Gardens for Florida" and "Best Garden Color for Florida." This plant has a **low wind tolerance.**

Bischofia (*Bischofia javanica*)
Zones 9b to 11.

This tree is brittle, invasive, messy, and provides shade so dense that not much grows underneath its foliage. These trees were badly damaged in Ft. Myers during hurricane Charley with winds

of only 90 mph. If you have one of these, get rid of it before it gets rid of you! This tree has a **low wind tolerance**.

Black Olive (*Bucida buceras):*
Zones 10 to 11.

As you can see from the photo, this tree broke up badly in even 80 mph winds. Black olives are commonly planted throughout south Florida. The leaves stain whatever they land on. The shade they cast is so dense that not much grows underneath. They drop leaves constantly. And they break apart in storms with winds as low as 60 mph. What's not to like? According to Dr. Mary Duryea's survey of homeowners after hurricane Andrew (145 mph), 68% of the black olives were left standing. Uprooting was the most common type of failure in these cat 5 winds. Black olives were one of the five species that did the most property damage in Andrew (15). They have a **low wind tolerance** because even though it takes a lot of wind to blow them over, they show substantial crown damage in cat 1 storms.

Blolly (*Guapira discolor):* Zones 9b
to 11. The Palm Beach Chapter of the Florida Native Plant Society had three 'good' and two 'ok' reports on this tree's performance during Frances and Jeanne. The general consensus of the group was that it did well. The winds in the county ranged from about 50 to 100 mph during these two storms (19). I would love to have more data about

how more of these trees did in more wind. This one is impossible to classify because of so little data.

Bloodberry (*Cordia globosa):*
Zones 10-11. The Palm Beach Chapter of the Florida Native Plant Society had five 'good' and four 'ok' reports on this plant's performance during Frances and Jeanne. The general consensus of the group was that it did well. The winds in the county ranged from about 50 to 100 mph during these two storms (19). Once again, I need more data on this plant to classify its wind tolerance but I'm happy that at least we all know something about its wind tolerance!

Blue Daze (*Evolvulus glomeratus):*
Zones 10 to 11 as a perennial. All reports found that this plant did well with wind but poorly with flooding. For more information about this plant, see "Easy Gardens for Florida." It has a **high wind tolerance**.

Bottlebrush (*Callistemon spp.*)
Zones 9 to 11.

According to Pam Brown of the Pinellas County Extension (near Tampa), she saw some bottlebrush blown out of the ground, completely or partially, even though that area only experienced cat 1 winds (3). Tom MacCubbin reports that they suffered minimal damage in Orlando with the three hurricanes it experienced in 2004 (31). The winds in Orlando probably also didn't exceed cat 1 force.

Information From Throughout the State

According to Dr. Mary Duryea's survey after hurricane Andrew (145 mph), 52% were left standing (15). This tree has a **medium wind tolerance.** Photo by Joleen King.

Bougainvillea *(Bougainvillea spp.):* Zones 9 to 11.

I reported a lot of information about this plant in my "Best Garden Color for Florida" book. The plant itself tolerated the wind well. When trained as a tree, it blew over in very low winds, like 40 mph, but recovered easily after staking. Some plants had their leaves completely blown off, but they came back quickly. These differences make this plant hard to classify as low, medium, or high.

Bromeliads

All reports on bromeliads are good, even from people in areas that measured over 120 mph. The bromeliads with thick leaves, like the aechmea shown above, have at a minimum, a **high wind tolerance**. See the indexes of "Easy Gardens for Florida", "Best Garden Color for Florida", and "Container Gardens for Florida" for more information on some great bromeliads.

Bulbine *(Bulbine frutescens):* Zones 10 to 11.

I listed this groundcover as having a medium wind tolerance in the "Best Garden Color for Florida" book. I will change it to **high** for the next printing. This plant did extremely well in winds of up to 90 mph, not even losing its flowers!

Buttonwood *(Conocarpus erectus):* Zones 10b to 11.

I didn't get many reports on this tree's performance, but it has a history of **high wind tolerance**. It has a green and a silver cultivar. I saw a number of small silver buttonwoods on the ground, but I think that was because they were newly planted. I would like to hear more; if anyone knows more about this tree's performance, email me at colorgdn@aol.com. For more information about this plant, see "Easy Gardens for Florida."

Carrotwood *(Cupaniopsis anacardio):* Carrotwood is an invasive exotic tree, meaning that it is crowding out native plants in our forests. It is a pain in the neck because it drops messy seeds that sprout, creating a little invasive forest in your front yard! I didn't hear many reports of trees down, however, and because of this lack of information, I cannot classify this plant.

Cedar, Southern Red *(Juniperus silicicola):* Dr. Mary Duryea reported significant crown damage in Erin (85 mph winds), but only 8% fell. Forty percent fell after Opal (125 mph winds). Most often, they broke off at the stem (14). Tom MacCubbin from Orlando (70 mph winds) that reported older specimens were the most affected. Their trunks were twisted and distorted, and they often fell. Since this plant shows significant damage in cat 1 storms, I am giving it a **low wind tolerance**.

Chenille, Dwarf or Trailing *(Acalypha pendula):* Zones 7 to 11. All reports say this one did well. I saw dwarf chenille looking good at the Breakers Resort at Palm Beach four weeks after Jeanne hit with winds of 100 mph. This plant has at least a **high wind tolerance** provided it is planted in the ground. Unfortunately, our only experience with dwarf chenille comes from planting it in the ground. Considering it is such a low plant and the the winds are always much lower on the ground, we don't know how it would perform if it were planted higher - in a planter on a balcony - for example. See "Easy Gardens for Florida" and "Container Gardens for Florida" for more information about this plant.

Wind-Tolerance of Florida Plants

Cherry Laurel, *(Prunus caroliniana):* Zones 8 to 9.

This plant was rated as one of the worst two by Dr. Mary Duryea after her study of the panhandle after Opal and Erin (14). Tom MacCubbin reported "limb damage and many blown over in Charley, Frances, and Jeanne" in winds of about 70 mph in Orlando (31). Pam Brown from the Pinellas County Extension saw several cherry laurels twisted and broken off in their 60 to 70 mph winds (3). I also received reports of many down in west Volusia county, where the winds were probably in the 70 mph range. Cherry laurels have a **low wind tolerance.** Photo by Joan Brookwell.

Cinnamon Bark *(Canella alba):* Zones 10 to 11. The Palm Beach Chapter of the Florida Native Plant Society had three 'good' reports on this plant's performance during Frances and Jeanne. The winds in the county ranged from about 50 to 100 mph during these two storms (19). With this limited information, I cannot classify the plant, but I'm happy that we have some information about how it performs.

Citrus
Citrus do fairly well in cat 1 or cat 2 storms; but they don't fare well in winds that are stronger. They have a **medium wind tolerance.**

Cocoplum *(Chrysobalanus icaco):* Zones 9b to 11.

(The red-tipped is more cold sensitive than the green.) Cocoplum is primarily used as a hedge in the landscape. In its native habitat, it grows into a small tree. The Palm Beach Chapter of the Florida Native Plant Society had eleven 'good' and three 'ok' reports on the hedges' performance. The tree tended to bend over, although the leaves showed no damage at all during Frances and Jeanne. The winds in this county ranged from about 50 to 100 mph during these two storms (19). This plant has a **medium wind tolerance.**

Coleus *(Solenostemon scuttelariodes):* Zone: Grown throughout Florida as an annual. This plant did

surprisingly well near the worst areas hit by Jeanne and Frances. The photo (above) was taken at the Breakers Resort (100 mph winds, at least) just

a few weeks after Jeanne. Lloyd Singleton, from the Breakers, said they looked as good as new right after the storms! I don't know if this is because of their superior wind tolerance or the fact that the wind speed is very low that close to the ground, even in a hurricane, . See "Best Garden Color for Florida" and "Container Gardens for Florida" for lots more information about coleus.

Coralbean *(Erythrina herbacea):* Zones 8 to 11. The Palm Beach Chapter of the Florida Native Plant Society had four 'good', two 'ok', three 'so-so' reports on this plant's performance during Frances and Jeanne. The winds in the county ranged from about 50 to 100 mph (19). I don't have enough information to classify the coralbean, but I'm glad to have something! Does anyone have more information?

Crepe Myrtle *(Lagerstroemia indica):* Zones 7 to 10b.

Crepe myrtles are a star in storms. I had great reports from all over the state. One homeowner from near Pensacola reported that they lost oaks, pines, and poplars but the crepe myrtle did well (17). Pam Brown of the Pinellas County Extension said that she saw no damage on these trees with their 70-75 mph winds (3). Dr. Mary Duryea of University of Florida calls the crepe myrtle "quite good" for wind tolerance (16). According to

Information From Throughout the State

Teresa Watkins of Florida Yards and Neighborhoods in Orlando, "My experiences with the crepe myrtles were that they survived well if they had not been trimmed improperly. The ones on my property all did beautifully but several streets over, crepe myrtles that had been hatracked in previous years didn't make it due to the heavy branches at the top"(51). Holly Shackelford from the Charlotte County Extension reported that three months after cat 4 Charley the crepe myrtles were "battered, but didn't uproot or have any broken branches. They are leaning and leafless at this point."(47). Larry Williams reported that crepe myrtles did well in Ivan, holding up to its 125 mph winds. He only saw a few slightly uprooted other than those right along the coast (where some were lost). I classified this plant as having a medium wind tolerance in my "Best Garden Color for Florida" book. However, with these glowing reports, it clearly has a **high wind tolerance**.

Crepe Myrtle, Queen's

(Lagerstroemia speciosa): Zones 10 to 11.

One homeowner from Ft. Lauderdale (60 mph winds) reported a queen's crepe lost half its canopy but is coming back (17). I lost one that was planted in a container. Since we have so little data on this plant, I cannot classify it. For more information on this beautiful tree, see "Best Garden Color for Florida."

Crotons *(Codiaeum spp)* Zones 10 to 11.

Crotons did amazingly well. Don Wacker, living on a barrier island off Vero Beach that received some of the worst winds from Frances (cat 2) and Jeanne (cat 3) reports that his all fared well. His fire crotons were "exposed directly to wind and no damage at all" (50). The crotons in our trial gardens looked like nothing had happened to them! Crotons have a **high wind tolerance**. For more information about these great plants, see "Easy Gardens for Florida", "Best Garden Color for Florida", and "Container Gardens for Florida."

Crown of Thorns *(Euphorbia millii)*: Zones 10 to 11.

I heard conflicting reports about this plant's performance. The Breakers Resort at Palm Beach, which received winds of at least 100 mph, told me that theirs (above) did great. A landscaper who has a lot of clients further west, where some flooding occurred, said

that all of his died. My guess is that this plant has a **high wind tolerance** but no tolerance for any flooding at all. For more information about this plant, see "Easy Gardens for Florida" and "Container Gardens for Florida."

Cypress, Bald *(Taxodium distichum)*: Zones 4-10.

This photo was taken by Daniel Culbert shortly after Charley - in Arcadia, which was clobbered by this hurricane. You can see it is still standing! Tom MacCubbin from the Orange County Extension says that the bald cypress is a very strong tree (31). The Palm Beach Chapter of the Florida Native Plant Society had all 'good' reports on this tree's performance during Frances and Jeanne. The winds in the county ranged from about 50 to 100 mph during these two storms (16). Dr. Mary Duryea of the University of Florida says that the bald cypress is all in all a sturdy tree. But she went on to say the top sometimes breaks off of the large trees, and it may uproot along lakes and ponds (16). The USDA lists this in their most wind-tolerant category. Holly Shackelford of the Charlotte County Extension reports a few broken

Wind-Tolerance of Florida Plants

branches, but other than that, the bald cypress made it through cat 4 Charley just fine (39). Bald cypress has a **high wind tolerance**. It is also useful in areas prone to flooding because it falls less than most other species in wet soil.

Cypress, Pond *(Taxodium ascendens):* Zones 5-10.

I saw a number of these trees down in Palm Beach County in 80 mph winds. **Medium wind tolerance**.

Cypress, Leyland *(x Cupressocyparis leylandii):*

Zones 6 to 10. The above photo of this plant was taken in Arcadia by Dan Culbert after cat 4 Charley, and the plant looks untouched. Larry Williams from Okaloosa County revealed that his leyland cypress did not fare as well in Ivan, 125 mph winds. He goes on to say that "a good number were significantly uprooted and many were split and injured to the point that they had to be removed" (53). I'm not classify-

ing this plant because I'd like more information, but this is a good start.

Dogwood *(Cornus florida):* Zones 7 to 9a.

This is a medium tree, normally reaching 20 to 30 feet in height. Although it is susceptible to multiple pests and is not drought tolerant, it received glowing reports from the panhandle about dogwoods after Ivan. They also did extremely well in Opal (cat 3) and Erin (cat 1). Dr. Mary Duryea reports that "most all were left standing" after the two storms with little crown damage. However, she concluded that this tree met its match in Camille (cat 5), where it was reported to be easily uprooted (14). Since cat 5 hurricanes are so rare, the dogwood is a real winner for central and north Florida. It has a **high wind tolerance.** Photos by Doug Caldwell.

Draceana reflexa 'Song of India' *(Draceana reflexa):* Zone 10 to 11. This is a very wind-tolerant,

easy plant that breezed through days of 80 mph winds. For more information on this plant, see "Best Garden Color for Florida." This plant has a **high wind tolerance**.

Elms, Drake or Chinese *(Ulmus parvifolia)* Zones 5 to 9.

Tom MacCubbin from Orlando reported that drake elms are shallow rooted and blew over easily in their 70 mph winds (31). I also received a few reports that it has brittle wood. And many people reported this tree down in Tampa, which had winds of 60 to 70 mph. The drake elm has a **low wind tolerance**. Photo by Leon Konieczny.

Eucalyptus *(Eucalyptus spp):*

This photo of rainbow eucalyptus was taken by Linda Seals from Mounts Botanical Garden in West Palm Beach. It fell in winds of about 80 to 100 mph. I received two other negative reports on eucalyptus. A homeowner from Okaloosa County (wind estimate 100 mph) said that many eucalyptus trees were uprooted (14). Another homeowner from south Georgia (wind speed, unknown) reported most of the eucalyptus in his neighborhood were down (17). Most of the trees near me (80 mph) did not fall but suffered a moderate amount of crown damage. This tree is difficult to classify because of only three reports, but it has either a **low** or **medium** wind tolerance.

Ficus *(Ficus benjamina)* Zones 10 to 11.

This ficus tree was one of the most destructive in south Florida. It has two big problems in dealing with wind, shallow roots and a dense canopy. According to Dr. Mary Duryea's survey of homeowners after hurricane Andrew (145 mph), less than 50% of these trees were left standing (15). I even had reports of these trees toppling over in only 60 mph winds (17). When these trees fall, they uproot and expose huge root balls that are not only destructive but also very expensive to remove. On the other hand, ficus that were professionally trimmed did much better than those that were allowed to develop dense canopies that could behave like sails in the wind - at least in situations of 100 mph or less. Ficus also did better if their aerial roots were allowed to grow into the ground to increase their stability. However, if I had a ficus tree within falling distance of my home, I would remove it, regardless of the cost. They are a very dangerous risk to have near buildings. See more about ficus on pages 48 and 49. They obviously have a **low wind tolerance**. If you like the look of a ficus, try the native strangler fig *(Ficus aurea)*.

Ficus, Green Island *(Ficus microcarpa 'Green Island'):*

Zones 10b to 11. This shrub did very well with high wind and salt, as shown in the above photo, taken at the Breakers Resort at Palm Beach, which experienced winds of at least 100 mph. This plant is located about fifty feet off the beach, so it received a lot of salt spray as well. Based on this information, I am quite comfortable giving green island ficus a **high wind tolerance**. It may even have a **very high wind tolerance**.

Fiddlewood *(Citharexylum fruticosum):* Zones 9b to 11.
The Palm Beach Chapter of the Florida Native Plant Society had six 'good', one 'ok', one 'so-so' and two 'it's-a-disaster' reports on this plant's performance during Frances and Jeanne. The winds in the county ranged from about 50 to 100 mph (19). Although this isn't enough information to classify this plant, it is a start!

Firebush *(Hamelia patens):* Zones 8b to 11.

The Palm Beach Chapter of the Florida Native Plant Society had seven good, six 'ok', ten 'so-so', and two 'it's-a-disaster' reports on this plant's

performance during Frances and Jeanne (19). This wide range of experience expresses different sizes and shapes of the plant. For example, a small, shrubby firebush would do well in high winds. However, a tall firebush with thick trunks would break up because the thicker wood is brittle. Whatever happens during the storm, the plant regenerates quickly. Let's keep planting this one for our butterflies! Firebush has a **medium wind tolerance** if it is maintained under four feet. For more information about this great butterfly plant, see "Easy Gardens for Florida."

Firespike *(Odontonema strictum):* Zones 7 to 11.

Firespike blew over in the 80 mph winds at my house, and I received other reports of it doing the same thing in 120 mph winds. However, it came back nicely after a hard cut back, flowering within about two months of the storms. This was a pleasant surprise because it was flowering before the storms and I had no idea it would recover and bloom again so quickly. Firespike has a **low wind tolerance**. For more information on this great hummingbird plant, see "Easy Gardens for Florida" and "Best Garden Color for Florida."

Wind-Tolerance of Florida Plants

Flax *(Dianella ensifolia):*

I was delighted to see how well this plant did at the Breakers Resort in Palm Beach, which had winds of about 100 mph. See the above photo to see that this plant didn't even know there was a hurricane! I also had several reports of this plant doing very well in nurseries that had substantial losses from other landscape plants in Frances and Jeanne. Flax has a **high wind tolerance**.

Floss Silk Tree *(Chorisia speciosa or Ceiba speciosa):* Zone 9 to 11.

The floss silk tree is a gorgeous tree with a lousy wind tolerance. Just how lousy is up to debate. Surveys showed anywhere from 50% to 100% of these trees died after hurricane Andrew within the affected area. The tree is so beautiful, however, that it certainly still has a place. Just don't plant it close enough to fall on anything important. For more information, see "Best Garden Color for Florida." This tree has a **low wind tolerance**.

Geiger Tree, Orange *(Cordia sebestena):* Zones 10 to 11.
This is a great native tree with lovely orange flowers. I wish I had more data on its wind tolerance. It has a reputation for **high wind tolerance**, but I don't know how much it breaks in the winds. The Palm Beach Chapter of the Florida Native Plant Society had four good, four 'ok', and three so-so reports on this tree's performance during Frances and Jeanne. The winds in the county ranged from about 50 to 100 mph during these two storms (19). Learn more about this tree in "Easy Gardens for Florida."

Golden Penda Tree
(Xanthostemon chrysanthus):
One secondhand report stated that one of these trees suffered no damage on a site in Palm Bay (wind estimate, 120 mph) while many other species split or fell over (17). Since this is the only report I have on this tree, I will reserve judgement on it, but will plant one in our trial gardens to learn more about it.

Golden Rain Tree *(Koelreuteria elegans):* Zones 6 to 11.

I had many reports from different areas about this tree's brittleness. One report came from west Volusia County, where the winds were probably 60 to 70 mph, told of golden rain trees snapping in half or losing major limbs (17). This tree has a **low wind tolerance**.

Golden Shower Tree *(Cassia fistula):* Zones 10 to 11.

I only have one report on this tree, a person from Ft. Myers (estimated winds 90 mph) said that of 12 out of 14 golden shower trees came down. The trees were twenty years old (17). This leads me to believe that it has a low wind tolerance, but I need more data to know for sure. For more information about this tree, see "Best Garden Color for Florida."

Grapefruit *(Citrus x paradisi)*
Zones 9 to 11. According to Dr. Mary Duryea's survey of homeowners after hurricane Andrew (145 mph), less than 42% of these trees were left standing (15). The tree remained standing in 80 mph winds of Frances and Jeanne. So, somewhere between 80 and 145 mph, the grapefruits start to fall. I am going to guestimate that this one has a **medium wind tolerance**.

Information From Throughout the State

Gumbo Limbo *(Bursera simaruba):* Zones 9b to 11.

Most gumbo limbos do well in hurricanes. The top photo shows what most of them looked like in the Sanibel-Captiva area after Charley. They lost their leaves and smaller branches but the structure of the tree remained standing. The bottom photo shows that hurricanes are unpredictable - this gumbo limbo fell in the same area that most others stood tall. These two photos are by Rusty Isler. In Dr. Mary Duryea's survey of homeowners after hurricane Andrew, this was one of the top three trees with 84% still standing after the storm. (15). The Palm Beach Chapter of the Florida Native Plant Society had twelve 'good' and five only 'ok' reports on this tree's performance during Frances and Jeanne.

The winds in the county ranged from about 50 to 100 mph during these two storms (19). I had many glowing reports from throughout the southern parts of the state about this tree's ability to stay upright during hurricanes. But it broke up a lot, and some people were left with a stick coming out of the ground where they used to have a big shade tree. But all in all, it did very well, especially in Sanibel and Captiva, which were two of the hardest hit areas of the 2004 hurricanes. However, I did hear of two gumbo limbos dying in Boca Raton, where the winds probably didn't top 50 mph. This tree merits a **high wind tolerance**. For more information about this gorgeous tree, see "Easy Gardens for Florida."

Heliconia *(Heliconia spp):* Zones 10a to 11.

I had reports of this plant getting shredded in 60 mph winds. But the roots stayed alive and re-sprouted soon after. I had some in containers that were well-sheltered by my palms in the pool garden shown in the Page 109I. This plant has a **low wind tolerance**. For more information, see "Best Garden Color for Florida."

Hibiscus *(Hibiscus rosa-sinensis):* Zones 10a to 11. As I report in my

other books, hibiscus has good wind tolerance provided it is left in shrub form. When trimmed into a small tree, it falls over easily, uprooting. Don Wacker, living on a barrier island off Vero Beach that received some of the worst winds from Frances (cat 2) and Jeanne (cat 3) reports that one of his hibiscus trees snapped off 12 inches above the ground. He must have experienced winds well over 100 mph. However, his hibiscus stump began producing new leaves shortly, but it will be a shrub this time instead of a tree. If you want to grow a hibiscus as a tree, I recommend permanent staking. But since the natural shrub form of this plant does so well in wind, it deserves a **high wind tolerance**. For more information about hibiscus, see "Best Garden Color for Florida."

Wind-Tolerance of Florida Plants

Holly, Chinese *(Ilex cornuta):* Zones 7 to 9b. According to Peggy Dessaint, Manatee County Extension, a chinese holly hedge, four feet tall, made it through 75 mph winds with no damage. It was fully exposed to the winds. (13). Since that is all the information I have on this plant, I'll wait for more before classifying its wind tolerance.

Holly, Dahoon *(Ilex cassine):* Zones 7 to 10.

The Palm Beach Chapter of the Florida Native Plant Society had nine 'good', five 'ok', and three 'so-so' reports on this plant's performance during Frances and Jeanne. They felt the difference in performance was due to the placement of the trees. The winds in the county ranged from about 50 to 100 mph during these two storms (19). According to Peggy Dessaint, Manatee County Extension, a 12 foot tall dahoon holly made it through 75 mph winds with no damage. It was fully exposed to the winds and located on a water-logged site near some wax myrtles that were lifted right out of the ground. (13). Adrian Hunsberger of the Miami-Dade County Extension, stated that dahoon hollies have a medium wind resistance. She says that 50% to 75% were left standing after Andrew's 145 mph winds (25). Holly

Shackelford of the Charlotte County Extension said the dahoons "came through okay" in cat 4 Charley (47). This plant deserves a **high wind tolerance** classification, which translates into the fact that it takes cat 3 winds fairly well.

Hong Kong Orchid *(Bauhinia blakeana):* Zones 9 to 11.

Although this tree has a **low wind tolerance**, it recovers quickly when re-staked. Its intolerance to wind could be due to the thickness of the canopy. I wonder if it was routinely and professionally trimmed if it would do better. According to Dr. Mary Duryea's survey of homeowners after hurricane Andrew (145 mph), less than 50% of these trees were left standing (15). An old Hong Kong orchid was reported uprooted in 84 mph winds at Vanderbilt Beach near Naples (17). Even though it lacks wind tolerance, it has lovely flowers. Just don't plant one in a location where it could fall on something important! To learn more, see "Easy Gardens for Florida."

Ironwood, Black *(Krugiodendron ferreum):* Zones 9b to 11.

(Top photo by Joan Brookwell.) I am intrigued by the possibilities for this small tree which eventually grows to 20 feet tall. It could be a storm superstar, one of the few that survive the really big ones. The Palm Beach Chapter of the Florida Native Plant Society had eight 'good' and one 'ok' reports on this trees's performance during Frances and Jeanne. The group reported that this tree had 'virtually no damage'. It ranked at the top of their discussion of hundreds of native plants. The winds in the county ranged from about 50 to 100 mph during these two storms (19). According to Roger Hammer, in Castellow Hammock in south Miami-Dade, none of these trees fell during hurricane Andrew. Castellow Hammock received the worst wind of the north wall of hurri-

Information From Throughout the State

cane Andrew, probably more than 150 mph. Roger says this tree's success could have something to do with its small stature (22). I have never had one of these, but will be planting clumps of them in my trial gardens to try as wind screens. I have heard that the fallen berries are a nuisance. This tree has at least a **high wind tolerance**, and may be amongst the few with a **very high wind tolerance**.

Ixora *(Ixora spp):* Zones 10 to 11.

The top photo by Rusty Isler shows ixora looking pretty good with a damaged building behind it! Don Wacker, living on a barrier island off Vero Beach that received some of the worst winds from Frances (cat 2) and Jeanne (cat 3) reports that his ixora "fared well and did not lose a leaf!" I know this plant has at least a **medium wind tolerance**, and it could have a **high**

wind tolerance. For more information about this plant, see "Easy Gardens for Florida."

Jacaranda *(Jacaranda mimosifolia):* Zones 9 to 11.

These two photos by Linda Seals of Mounts Botanical Gardens show that their jacarandas were broken and twisted by the 80 to 100 mph winds of Frances. According to Pam Brown, all of the jacaranda trees at Florida Botanical Gardens in Pinellas County (70-75 mph winds) had branches broken by the winds (3). A Ft. Lauderdale lady reported her jacaranda shredded in 60 mph winds (17). According to

Teresa Watkins of Florida Yards and Neighborhoods in Orlando, "There was a "jewel" of a jacaranda on Highway 441 north of Tavares on Lake Eustis (in a little boat marina inlet) that was over 40' in height. With the colder temperatures in Lake County, this Jacaranda was a rarity this far north , surviving decades of traumatic freezes due to the warmth of the lake waters. People would gape and stare as they drove by on the highway when it was in full purple plumage. With the hurricanes (don't know if it was Frances or Charley), the jacaranda split in two with half of the tree still standing and the other half (two huge branches) straddling across the cove in the water." (42a). Based on these accounts, this tree has a **low wind tolerance**. See "Best Garden Color for Florida" for more information about this tree.

Jamaica Caper *(Capparis cynophallophora):* Zones 9b to 11. The Palm Beach Chapter of the Florida Native Plant Society had 15 'good' and six 'ok' reports on this plant's performance during Frances and Jeanne. The winds in the county ranged from about 50 to 100 mph during these two storms (19). I need more data before classifying this beautiful native shrub, but am confident that is has at least a **medium wind tolerance**.

Jamaica Dogwood *(Piscidia piscipula)* Zones 9a to 11. The Palm Beach Chapter of the Florida Native Plant Society had one 'ok' and two 'so-so' reports on this tree's performance during Frances and Jeanne. They concluded that this tree breaks up in wind. The winds in this county ranged from about 50 to 100 mph during these two storms (19). I had reports from Sanibel (145 mph) that these trees did indeed break up, but recovered quickly. I hesitate to classify this tree without more data.

Wind-Tolerance of Florida Plants

Java Plum *(Syzigium cumini):* This tree is an invasive exotic, crowding out our natural areas. It is also has a very **low wind tolerance**. Don't plant this one, and if you have one in your yard, consider removing it. If it is within falling distance of your house, it could be a real danger.

Lignum Vitae *(Guaiacum sanctum):* Zones 10 to 11.

Roger Hammer, noted author and naturalist from Castellow Hammock in Miami-Dade County, has aptly named the lignum vitae "the Lamborghini of plants". Like the car, this plant is small, attractive, and expensive. But expensive in the plant world is not the same as in the world of luxury cars.

You can get a four-foot specimen for a few hundred dollars at the time of the printing of this book. It's problem is that it grows to it's eventual height very slowly. But talk about wind tolerant! According to Dr. Mary Duryea's survey after hurricane Andrew (145 mph), she had reports of only 6 or 7 of this species, which may not be enough for a true scientific survey. However, 100% were still standing after the storm (15). This tree has always had a reputation for being unbelievably strong. The Palm Beach Chapter of the Florida Native Plant Society had five 'good' and one 'ok' report on this tree's performance during Frances and Jeanne. The winds in the county ranged from about 50 to 100 mph during these two storms. This lovely small tree deserves at least a **high wind tolerance**, and maybe even a **very high** ranking. The top photo is from Bill Reeve from Botanical Visions and the close up is by Gene Joyner.

Lime, Key *(Citrus aurantifolia 'Key Lime'):* According to Dr. Mary Duryea's survey of homeowners after hurricane Andrew (145 mph), 75% of these trees fell (15). A homeowner from Vanderbilt Beach (84 mph winds) reported that half of her key lime tree was broken (14). Based on these reports, this plant gets a **low wind tolerance**. Plant this one in a protected location.

Lime, Wild *(Zanthoxylum fagara):* Zones 9a to 11. The Palm Beach Chapter of the Florida Native Plant Society had five good and four ok reports on this tree's performance during Frances and Jeanne. They concluded that this tree did pretty well. The winds in this county ranged from about 50 to 100 mph during these two storms (19). Based on these reports, and the consensus of citrus as a whole, this tree gets a **medium wind tolerance**.

Loquat *(Eriobotrya japonica)* According to Dr. Mary Duryea's survey of homeowners after hurricane Andrew (145 mph), 91% of these trees fell but her sample size was small (15). I had a report from Volusia County, where winds probably reached 60 to 70 mph, of many loquats leaning (17). Many reports came in from Palm Beach County (winds 50 - 100 mph) of severe damage to loquat trees. This tree has a **low wind tolerance**.

Magnolia, Southern *(Magnolia grandiflora):* Zones 7 to 10b.

Glowing reports came in from throughout the state regarding this tree's wind tolerance. Dr. Mary Duryea reports that less than 10% had significant crown damage) in Erin and Opal, which means that it does well in up to cat 3 storms (14). Tom MacCubbin reported very little damage in

Orlando's 70 mph winds (31). I had a report from west Volusia County, where the winds were in the 60 to 70 mph range, that these trees were one of the best (17). This tree rates at least a **high wind tolerance**, and possibly a **very high wind tolerance**. For more information about this great tree, see "Best Garden Color for Florida."

Magnolia, Sweetbay *(Magnolia virginiana):* Zones 8 to 10.

The Palm Beach Chapter of the Florida Native Plant Society had six 'good' reports on this tree's performance during Frances and Jeanne. Since 'good' was the best they could choose, this plant was one of the few trees in their discussions to receive perfect marks. The winds in the county ranged from about 50 to 100 mph during these two storms (19). One report from Sebring said that this plant suffered a lot of damage, more than most other native trees. With no more data, this tree is difficult to classify. This photo of a small sweetbay was taken by Trent Roller at his tree farm, Heartwood Nursery, 931-934-2953.

Mahoe, Seaside *(Thespesia populnea)* This is one of the worst trees I have ever had because it spreads sideways wider and faster than any other i

have ever seen, killing whatever is underneath. It is also brittle, breaking easily in the wind. **Low wind tolerance.**

Mahogany *(Swietenia mahogani):* Zones 10b to 11.

I took the photos of these mahogany trees in a parking lot near my home shortly after Frances, when the winds didn't exceed 80 mph. Many professionals disagree about the wind tolerance of mahogany trees because it is a tree of extremes. The wood is quite brittle, so the branches break up and fall off in very low winds. The roots, however, are quite strong and they almost never uproot. Marilyn Steward (48) of Naples said that these trees lost quite a few branches there. The winds in Naples were not that high, about 60 mph, during Charley. Reports came in from Fort Lauderdale, where the winds can't have topped 60 mph, of major

limb damage (17). From Vanderbilt Beach, near Naples, where the winds were clocked at 84 mph, one homeowner said, "It snapped off huge major limbs from three large mahogany trees, completely destroying one of them" (17). The Palm Beach Chapter of the Florida Native Plant Society had five 'good', two 'ok', two 'so-so', and five 'it's-a-disaster' reports on this tree's performance during Frances and Jeanne. The winds in the county ranged from about 50 to 100 mph during these two storms (19). However, Dr. Mary Duryea's survey of homeowners after hurricane Andrew (145 mph winds) showed 75% of the mahoganies were still standing (15). Even though it still stands, the brittleness of the branches rates this one a **low wind tolerance**. For more information about this tree, see "Easy Gardens for South Florida."

Mango *(Mangifera indica):* Zones 10 to 11.

This photo was taken by Linda Seals from Mounts Botanical Gardens in West Palm Beach shortly after hurricane Frances. The winds reached about 80 to 100 mph at that location during that storm. Although mango trees broke up a lot, most survived the 2004 quartet. However, according to Crane, about 70% of the mango trees initially survived Andrew. But many of the survivors died and declined over the following four years (10). Dr. Mary Duryea's survey of homeowners after hurricane Andrew (145 mph winds) showed 60% of the mangoes were still standing but they were one of the five species that caused the most property damage. (15). A homeowner from Vanderbilt Beach (84 mph winds) reported her Edward mango blew over but was righted and staked (17). This tree has a **low wind tolerance**.

Maple, Japanese *(Acer palmatum):* Zones 5 to 9a.

This is a small tree that did very well in the 2004 hurricanes in the northern half of the state. It eventually grows to 20 feet, but most are smaller. This photo is by Daniel Culbert. **High wind tolerance**

Maple, Red *(Acer rubrum):* Zones 8 to 10b)

Red Maple seems to have a decent wind resistance in its branches, as Dr. Mary Duryea reports from her survey after Erin and Opal. She says that less than 10% had significant crown damage (over 50% branches broken) in those two storms, one of which was a cat 3 (14). However, I have a lot of reports that it blows over easily. Tom MacCubbin from Orlando (70 mph winds) states that this tree is "shallow rooted and usually blown over"(31). Jackie Dawson reports that a few large maples at her Boynton condo (winds 70 to 90 mph) fell. She stated that they were near the curb, which could have contributed to their falling. The USDA lists this as one of the least wind resistant trees. Holly Shackelford reports that the "majority uprooted and fell over or the major limbs broke" in cat 4 Charley (47). I'm giving this tree a **medium wind tolerance**, with cautions.

Marlbery *(Ardisia escallionioides):* Zones 9 to 11.

The Palm Beach Chapter of the Florida Native Plant Society had nine 'good', and two 'ok' reports on this plant's performance during Frances and Jeanne. The winds in the county ranged from about 50 to 100 mph during these two storms (19). This is not enough information to classify the tree, but it's a start!

Mastic *(Sideroxylon foetidissimim):* Zones 9b to 11.

I'm excited about the potential for this tree. It is quite large, too large for many residences. But we don't have many large shade trees other than the live oak that have a high wind tolerance in the southern end of the state. I don't have much experience with it, though, and will shortly purchase one for our trial gardens. The Palm Beach Chapter of the Florida Native Plant Society had four 'good' reports on this tree's performance during Frances and Jeanne. This was the highest mark a tree could get in their discussion. The winds in the county in which this report was generated ranged from about 50 to 100 mph during these two storms (19). Adrian Hunsberger of the Miami-Dade County Extension office, reports that mastics have a good wind tolerance. Since Adrian lived through hurricane Andrew (145 mph), I respect her opinion! This tree has at least a **high wind tolerance**.

Melaleuca *(Melaleuca quinquenervia):* Zones 10 to 11.

Talk about extreme reports! According to Dr. Mary Duryea's survey following hurricane Andrew (145 mph), 79% of these trees were left standing (15). The reason for this large survival rate may be that many of the melaleucas in Andrew's path were in dense forests, so dense that the winds would not have been too strong in the center. The trees protected each other. I also received reports from Tampa, where winds probably reached 60 to 70 mph, that the melaleucas were one of the worst trees. A report from near Tampa (60 mph sustained winds with gusts to 80) of two melaleuca trees falling on someone's roof (17). It looks like melaleucas have a low wind tolerance if they are planted alone. Melaleucas are one of our worst invasive exotic trees, meaning they crowd out our natural areas. This in itself is enough of a reason to remove them. But if you have one within falling distance of your house, it could pose quite a danger. **Low wind tolerance**.

Myrtle of the River *(Calyptranthes zuzygium):* Zones 10 to 11.

The Palm Beach Chapter of the Florida Native Plant Society had five 'good' and one 'so-so' report on this plant's performance during Frances and Jeanne. The winds in the county ranged from about 50 to 100 mph during these two storms (19). Although this is not enough to classify this plant, it's a start!

Necklace Pod *(Sophora tomentosa)* Zones 8b to 11.

The Palm Beach Chapter of the Florida Native Plant Society had five 'good', eight 'ok', and four 'so-so' reports on this plant's performance during Frances and Jeanne. The winds in the county ranged from about 50 to 100 mph during these two storms (19). Although this is not enough to classify this plant, it's a start!

Information From Throughout the State

Norfolk Island Pine *(Araucaria heterophylla):* Zones 9b to 11.

This tree, which resembles a large Christmas tree, lost many of its branches in even low winds. I also had reports of it blowing over. It has a **low wind tolerance**. But contrary to popular belief, the branches will grow back. See the last chapter for information about trimming this tree after the storm. The bottom photo is by Stephen Brown.

Oak, Laurel *(Quercus laurifolia):* Zones 8 to 10.

This tree surprised a lot of people in its performance during Florida's 2004 hurricanes - myself included. I had thought that, since it was a native oak (most of which are highly wind tolerant) that it would do just fine. However, the laurel oak was one of the three most destructive trees in Florida in 2004's four storms. Most of the older specimens are in central and north Florida, and they wreaked untold damage and misery on the poor people whose houses happened to be hit by them. According to Tom MacCubbin from Orlando, the ones most affected were usually over 40 years old. That is not too old for most trees, but laurel oaks are short-lived and lose their strength and stability faster than most other oaks. They have the awful combination of both brittle wood and shallow roots, so even if they don't fall, they break up a lot. Beth Bolles of Escambia County, which was ravaged by Ivan, said that the laurel oak was one of their worst trees (2). I also had a lot of reports of laurel oaks down in Tampa, where the winds were probably 60 to 70 mph. This tree is beginning to appear more and more in the south Florida landscapes, and is difficult to distinguish from the much-stronger live oak. If you don't know whether your tree is a live oak or laurel oak, look at the plant profiles of each of them in my "Easy Gardens for Florida" book. I have photos of the leaves and tell you how to differentiate one from the other. This tree is native to Florida, which shows that not all of our native trees are tolerant of high winds. Although I ranked this tree as having a medium wind tolerance in my "Easy Gardens for Florida" book, I will definitely change it to **low wind tolerance** for the next printing. If you have a laurel oak within falling distance of your home, remove it before the next storm season. The top photo is by Gene Joyner and the bottom two are by Dan Mullins.

Oak, Live *(Quercus virginiana):* Zones 5 to 11.

Barbara Hadsell, our research assistant, drove to Punta Gorda (where the eye of Charley passed over) to check out the oaks. She reported that some died, but they appeared to be just at ground zero, where Charley made landfall. A short distance from that, almost all of them were releafing three months after the storm (photos, above). These trees had been through winds of over 130 mph, and they were still standing! Their appearance shows why the live oak is consistently ranked as the most wind-tolerant shade tree that is widely planted in Florida. According to Dr. Mary Duryea, it even ranked as the top shade tree after hurricane Camille, which is the strongest hurricane on record to ever hit the United States. She goes on to state that this tree also did well in Opal and Erin, showing little crown damage (14). Dr. Duryea also reported that this tree survived the 145 mph winds of Andrew well, with 78% left standing after the storm. Considering the strength of Andrew, these are excellent numbers. Uprooting was the most common type of failure (15). Tom MacCubbin reported that this is a sturdy tree, with only limited branch damage in Orlando's three hurricanes of 2004 (31). Sherry Williams, in her study of Brevard County's landscape after the 2004 storms, reports that the live oak blows over if not given adequate room to spread and if planted in moist soils (54). Beth Bolles from Escambia County, which was ravaged by Ivan, reported that many live oaks were still standing, although there was some canopy damage (2). According to Mark Peters of McKee Botanical Garden (120-130 mph winds), the live oaks did better than any other tree (39). Since this tree has the ability to do that well after a cat 3, or even cat 4 storm, it deserves a **very high wind tolerance**. The only problem I have with live oaks is that they are so good we may end up with too many of them. This is not a healthy situation because having too many of one kind of tree is a vulnerable situation if they become susceptible to a pest. Even though this tree has a great tolerance for wind, it is such a large tree that it could fall in a cat 1 to cat 3 storm for the reasons stated in Chapter 3. Since this tree needs considerable room for its roots to spread, it may become unstable if planted on residential properties with small yards. Its height of over 40 feet also increases the danger of it falling on a nearby structure in a hurricane.

This oak is also susceptible to Sudden Oak Death, a new pest not yet established in Florida.

Oak, Sand Live *(Quercus geminata):* Zones 8 to 10a.

This is a tree that is smaller than the live oak (about 20 to 30 feet tall) but seems to share its great wind tolerance. According to Dr. Mary Duryea, it did well in Opal and Erin and generally handles hurricane force winds extremely well. She says their wind tolerance is increased if they are used in groups (16). Adrian Hunsberger from the Miami-Dade County Extension says that these oaks are in the most wind-tolerant category (25). Larry Williams from Okaloosa County (Ivan, 125 mph), reports that "this tree did quite well, even along the coast. Very storm resistant" (53). These trees have at least a **high wind tolerance** and possibly a **very high wind tolerance.** I have not had any experience with this tree, so it will be a new one in my trial garden. I wonder if it might be a good choice for many residents who want an oak but not one as large as a live oak. Apparently, this tree does stain sidewalks, like black olives, but that is the only negative I know about so far. Photo by Joan Brookwell.

Information From Throughout the State

Oak, Water *(Quercus nigra):* Zones 7 to 9b.

Sherry Williams from Brevard County reports that water oaks have brittle wood and that they are not recommended (54). Beth Bolles of Escambia County, which was ravaged by Ivan, reported numerous uprooted water oaks. She said it was one of their worst trees (2). The Santa Rosa County Public Works Department told us that water oaks, along with laurel oaks, accounted for a substantial percentage of the vegetative debris in the county. This tree has a **low wind tolerance**, and may be one of the worst. Top photo by Joan Brookwell; bottom photo by Gene Joyner.

Orange, Navel *(Citrus sinensis):* Zones 9 to 11. According to Dr. Mary Duryea's survey of homeowners after hurricane Andrew (145 mph), 66% of these trees were left standing (15). Orange trees have a **medium wind tolerance**.

Palm, Alexander *(Ptycosperma elegans):* Zones 10 to 11.

According to Dr. Mary Duryea's survey of homeowners after hurricane Andrew (145 mph), 41% of these trees were left standing (15). These palms have a **medium wind tolerance**.

Palm, Areca *(Dypsis lutescens):* Zones 10b to 11.

This palm stays in the ground well during hurricanes but the fronds get quite torn up. I rated it with a low wind tolerance in my "Easy Gardens for Florida" book because of the dam-

age to the fronds. But I saw some photos of areca palms in Punta Gorda that took over 130 mph winds without uprooting. (They are shown in the photo taken by Allan Theisen.) For that reason, I believe this palm has at least a **medium wind tolerance**.

Palm, Canary Island Date *(Phoenix canariensis):*

Zones 9a to 11. All sources report that this palm has a **very high tolerance for wind**. It looked almost untouched after cat 4 winds hit in Arcadia, as shown by the photo (above) by Dan Culbert.

Palm, Cardboard, or Zamia *(Zamia furfuracea):* Zones 9b to 11.

This plant has had a reputation for toughness for years, so it is no surprise that all reports show its wind tolerance to be excellent, even at 100 mph +. This plant has at least a **high wind tolerance**. For more information about this useful plant, see "Easy Gardens for Florida."

Wind-Tolerance of Florida Plants

Palm, Cat *(Chamadorea cataractum):* Zones 10b to 11.

The only report I have on this palm was from the Breakers at Palm Beach, which received winds of at least 100 mph from Frances and Jeanne. They looked pretty torn up, as shown in the photo above. Based on this sighting, I'm giving this palm a **low wind tolerance**. For more information about this palm, see "Easy Gardens for Florida."

Palm, Chinese Fan *(Livistona chinensis):* Zones 9b to 11.

I received a lot of conflicting information about this palm. Stephen Brown from Lee County reported a medium wind tolerance (4). Adrian Hunsberger of the Miami-Dade County extension office, categorized this palm as very wind-tolerant (25). I think the difference may be in the height of the palm. It is relatively slow-growing, staying thick and almost shrub-like for a number of years. Eventually, it grows quite tall. It must respond differently to

wind at different heights. I will not classify it until I have more data. For more information about this palm, see "Easy Gardens for Florida."

Palm, Christmas or Adonidia *(Adonidia merrillii):* Zones 10b to 11.

Stephen Brown from Lee County reported a high wind tolerance (4). This report agrees with all the other available data on this palm, which has a **high wind tolerance**.

Palm, Coconut *(Cocos nucifera):* Zones 10 to 11.

This photo was taken on Hutchinson Island, near where Frances and Jeanne

made landfall, about three months after the hurricanes. This palm is native to beach areas and usually stands through cat 4 storms, as shown on numerous photos of Sanibel and Captiva after cat 4 Charley. But I did get isolated reports of these trees falling in lesser winds. Mounts Botanical Gardens in West Palm Beach, which had winds of about 80 to 90 mph, had some uproot and others snap at the base. I reported in my "Easy Gardens for Florida" book that coconuts have high wind tolerance except for the Malayan dwarfs, which snap at the base. This could account for the problem at Mounts with the snapping, but not for the uprooting at such low winds. But the majority held up well in cat 4 winds. Frequently, they lost most of their fronds and look like sticks afterwards. The fronds grow back eventually. This palm has a **high wind tolerance**.

Palm, Date *(Phoenix dactylifera)* Zones 9b to 11.

This palm is similar to the Canary Island date palm. It is a beautiful, large-scale palm that makes a strong design statement in the landscape. Although it has some problems with pests and diseases, it has a **high wind tolerance**.

Palm, Foxtail *(Wodyetia bifucata):* Zones 10 to 11.

This photo was taken near Punta Gorda by Allan Theisen. He took the photo shortly after Charley during which this palm experienced winds of around 130 mph. Since this palm is relatively new to Florida, the 2004 hurricanes were our first chance to see how they did in a lot of wind. Overall, they did very well. Don Wacker, living on a barrier island off Vero Beach that received some of the worst winds from Frances (cat 2) and Jeanne (cat 3) reported that his were just planted in March of 2004 but they did well, although they required re-staking (50). This is surprising because newer palms are more susceptible to falling in windstorms than more established ones. Stephen Brown of Lee County stated that foxtails showed high wind tolerance in Charley (4). This plant has a **high wind tolerance** overall.

Palm, Paurotis *(Acoelorrhaphe wrightii)* Zone 10 to 11.

The Palm Beach Chapter of the Florida Native Plant Society had seven good reports and one only 'ok' report on this palm's performance during Frances and Jeanne. The winds in the county ranged from about 50 to 100 mph during these two storms (19). Holly Shackelford of the Charlotte County

Extension reports that these palms did well in cat 4 Charley (47). This palm has a **high wind tolerance**.

Palm, Pindo *(Butia capitata):* Zones 8 to 10.

Alan Theisen took this photo of a pindo palm in the Punta Gorda area after Charley. If it was still standing with a building torn up around it, it must be a strong tree! Beth Bolles of Escambia County, which was ravaged by Ivan, said this palm did fairly well (2). Larry Williams, from nearby Okaloosa County, reported that "most did quite well, but I did see some that were lost due to undermining of water directly along the coast."(53). The photo above was taken after Charley near Punta Gorda. This useful tree for colder areas appears to have a **high wind tolerance.**

Palm, Queen *(Syagrus romanzoffiana):* Zones 9b to 11.

While most palms do fairly well in high winds, queen palms are the exception. They blew down all over Florida. If you still have one within

falling distance of your house, consider removing it. Queen palms blow down more than most other commonly-planted Florida trees. They typically uproot rather than snapping at the trunk. According to Dr. Mary Duryea's survey after hurricane Andrew (145 mph), queen palms were one of the five species that did the most property damage (15). This palm has a **low wind tolerance**.

Palm, Roebelenii or Pygmy Date *(Phoenix roebelenii):* Zones 9 to 11.

This photo was taken by FEMA shortly after Andrew. The little pygmy date palm is surrounded by massive destruction, and it's still standing! This one is possibly the strongest plant around. Don Wacker, who lives near Vero Beach reported that they "fared perfectly - completely exposed to wind in excess of 120 mph and did not even require re-staking or pruning." (50). According to Dr. Mary Duryea's survey of homeowners after hurricane Andrew (145 mph), 100% of these trees were left standing (15). I have photos of sites from Andrew and Charley where buildings were blown apart and the pygmy date palms looked untouched! This is probably the most wind-tolerant plant in this book, and has a **very high wind tolerance**.

Wind-Tolerance of Florida Plants

Palm, Royal *(Roystonea elata)*: Zones 10 to 11.

These palms are native to Florida and take up to cat 4 winds with little trouble, other than the fact that they lose most of their fronds. Even in relatively low winds, the fronds show damage. Luckily, the majority of them recover. The Palm Beach Chapter of the Florida Native Plant Society had five 'good' reports and two that were only 'ok' in a county where the winds ranged from 50 to 100 mph during Frances and Jeanne (19). Many are reported recovering well from cat 4 Charley in Sanibel and Captiva, which were devastated by this storm. However, cat 5 winds can get the better of them. And when they fall in these very high winds, they typically uproot rather than breaking at the trunk. According to Dr. Mary Duryea's survey after hurricane Andrew (145 mph), royal palms were one of the five species that did the most property damage. The larger ones fell more than the smaller ones. The average height of a fallen royal was about 45 feet while the average height of a standing royal was about 30 feet (15). However, it takes a lot of wind to knock down a royal! Remember that cat 5 storms make up only 2% of all hurricanes. This palm has a **high wind tolerance**. The photo was taken by Rusty Isler after Charley.

Palm, Sabal *(Sabal palmetto)*: Zones 8 to 11.

This is our state tree, a title it especially deserves because it is one of our most wind-tolerant trees. The photo (by Allan Theisen) says it all - the trees looking quite healthy in the middle of debris from nearby torn-up buildings. According to Dr. Mary Duryea, it was the second most wind-resistant tree in the strongest hurricane on record, Camille (14). And it survived winds of at least 145 mph after Andrew. As a matter of fact, in Dr. Duryea's survey of homeowners after hurricane Andrew, the sabal palm was the second best survivor, with 93% still standing after the storm (15). Don Wacker's home on a barrier island off Vero Beach, which was hit by two hurricanes (120 mph), one tornado, and 30 inches of rain in a month, has a total of 21 sabal palms. Although some sport interesting new angles and are quite stripped, all are alive and well (50). I have several photos of sabal palms standing tall while buildings around them are destroyed. This is one of the few trees with a well-deserved **very high wind tolerance**.

Palm, Saw Palmetto *(Serenoa repens)*: Zones 8 to 11.

This is another one of Florida's wind superstars. It is native to Florida and should be used a lot more to create natural screens for more delicate plantings. Laura Tindall in Loxahatchee has a garden that was sheltered by palmettos. Her garden looked great after Frances and Jeanne (80 mph winds) while the gardens of her neighbor's were all torn up. These amazing palms showed <u>no damage</u> at Don Wacker's house (120 mph winds) on a barrier island off Vero Beach (50). According to Dr. Mary Duryea this is the "best palm around" (16). Stephen Brown from Lee County reports that palmettos did great during Charley (4). The Palm Beach Chapter of the Florida Native Plant Society had seventeen 'good' reports and only three 'ok' reports on this palm's performance during Frances and Jeanne. The winds in the county ranged from about 50 to 100 mph during these two storms (19). This palm has a **very high wind tolerance**.

Information From Throughout the State.

Palm, Senegal Date *(Phoenix reclinata):* Zones 9b to 11. According to Dr. Mary Duryea's survey of home-owners after hurricane Andrew (145 mph), 100% of these trees were left standing but she only had a sample size of 5. (15). I haven't had any more reports on this palm's performance, but since the other phoenix palms did so well, this one has at least a **high wind tolerance**.

Palm, Thatch, or Florida Thatch *(Thrinax radiata):* Zones 10b to 11.

All reports state that this palm has a **high wind tolerance**.

Palm, Washingtonia
(Washingtonia robusta) Zones 9 to 11. Sherry Williams from Brevard County reported a lot of these palms blown over (53). I also received a report from near Tampa (60 mph sustained winds, 80 mph gusts) of 24 of these palms down in one neighborhood (14). And Peggy Dessaint, Manatee County Extension Agent, reports a 30 foot tall specimen broken in half in the middle

of the trunk when fully exposed to 75 mph winds (13). Holly Shackelford of the Charlotte County Extension reported that Washingtonia palms did "very poorly" in cat 4 Charley. Many "broke in half or fell over" (47). I also received some good reports about Washingtonia palms and wonder if the shorter ones are more stable than the taller ones. Nonetheless, this palm obviously has a **low wind tolerance**.

Palmetto, see Palm, Saw Palmetto

Paradise Tree *(Simarouba glauca):* Zones 9b to 11.

The Palm Beach Chapter of the Florida Native Plant Society had three 'good', two 'ok', one 'so-so', and four 'it's-a-disaster' reports on this trees's performance during Frances and Jeanne. They concluded that this tree is brittle and breaks up in winds. The winds in this county ranged from about 50 to 100 mph during these two storms (19). However, the brittleness of the paradise tree does not cause it to fall. According to Roger Hammer, in Castellow Hammock in south Miami-Dade, none of these trees fell during hurricane Andrew. Castellow Hammock received the worst wind of the north wall of hurricane Andrew, probably more than 150 mph (22). Since this tree breaks up so badly, it has a **medium wind tolerance**. The photo was taken by Linda Seals of

Mounts Botanical Gardens in West Palm Beach. The tree broke in Frances with winds of 80 to 100 mph.

Pecan *(Carvia illindensis)* Zones 6 - 8. Pecan trees uproot and break up badly in hurricanes. Beth Bolles (2) of Escambia County, which was ravaged by Ivan, reported pecans to be amongst the worst trees for uprooting. **Low wind tolerance**.

Pentas *(Pentas lanceolata):* Zones 9 to 11as a perennial.

Kelly Mikesell (Tampa, 70 to 80 mph), reported that her cranberry pentas in a bed facing north didn't seem fazed at all. My guess is that, even though pentas are fairly wind-tolerant, they didn't get the full force of the wind at Kelly's house. Jeff Williams (52) said his pentas did well in Margate, where the winds were in the 60 mph range. But when the winds were higher, they were hurt. Don Wacker, living on a barrier island off Vero Beach that received some of the worst winds from Frances (cat 2) and Jeanne (cat 3) reports that he lost about half of her pentas died. This plant has a **medium wind toler-ance**.

Pigeon Plum *(Coccoloba diversi-folia):* Zones 9b to 11. The Palm Beach Chapter of the Florida Native Plant Society had eight 'good', five 'ok', and four 'so-so' reports on this tree's performance during Frances and Jeanne. The winds in the county ranged from about 50 to 100 mph dur-ing these two storms (19). I will with-hold classification of this tree until I have more data.

Wind-Tolerance of Florida Plants

Pine, Australian *(Casuarina spp):* Zones 9b to 11.

This tree is an invasive exotic, meaning it crowds out and threatens our natural areas. It also was one of the worst trees for falling over in the hurricanes of 2004. See pages 44-47 for more information on this tree. According to Dr. Mary Duryea's survey after hurricane Andrew (145 mph), this tree performed worse than any other, with only 4% left standing (15).

Pine, Sand *(Pinus clausa):* Zones 8 to 10a.

Sand pines are one of the worst trees for wind tolerance. According to Dr. Mary Duryea, "Sand pine should not be planted or allowed to grow to a large size near any dwelling. It's shal-low root system appears to make it extremely vulnerable to wind." She considered it one of the worst two in her survey of the panhandle after Erin (85 mph) and Opal (125 mph). A full 39% fell in Erin, which only had 85 mph winds! Only 46% were left after the next storm, Opal, hit a few weeks later (14). Sherry Williams from Brevard County said that this tree has "poor wind resistance." (54). And Beth Bolles (2) from Escambia County, which was ravaged by Ivan, reported that the sand pines turned brown. This color change could be due to the salt from the storm surge, but it can't be good news for this tree! Sand pines have a **low wind tolerance**. If you have one within falling distance of your house, it is dangerous. Photo by Gene Joyner.

Pines, Slash *(Pinus elliottii var. elliotti)*

Slash Pines have a good tolerance for wind in cat 1and cat 2 storms. Some of them snap but only a few percent. When the winds reach the cat 3 category, more of them snap, enough to make it dangerous to have one near your home. In cat 4 storms, even more of them snap. They have a deep tap root, so few of them uproot unless they are flooded. In cat 5 storms, strange things happen. According to Dr. Mary Duryea's study of homeowners after hurricane Andrew, 73% were left standing after the storm. The ones that fell typically broke at the trunk rather than uprooting. Larger pines were more likely to break than smaller ones. The average fallen slash pine was about 60 feet tall, while the average pine left standing was about 51 feet tall. Although 73% of these pines were left standing after the storm, most of them died during the following year, either to insect damage or hidden structural and root damage (15). Time will tell the survival rate of pines after the four storms of 2004. Slash pines suffer more damage if they are alone. The forest gives them natural protection, which is lost with single plantings. Beth Bolles (2) from Escambia County, which were ravaged by Ivan, reported numerous slash pines either uprooted or snapped along the trunk. Slash pines have a **medium wind tolerance**.

Plum, Chicasaw *(Prunus angustifolia):* Zones 5 to 9. Reports from west Volusia County, where winds probably reached 60 to 70 mph, stated that this plant either snapped in half or lost much of its crown. This is not enough information to classify this plant but is useful to have.

Plumbago *(Plumbago auriculata)* Zones 9b to 11.

Plumbago was a wonder shrub at my place. I didn't even have to cut it back after two hurricanes (80 mph), and it bloomed profusely within weeks of the storm. Kelly Mikesell from Tampa reported that hers needed a hard pruning. This plant has a **high wind tolerance**. For more information about this plant, see "Easy Gardens for Florida."

Information From Throughout the State.

Podocarpus *(Podocarpus macrophyllus):* Zones 10 to 11.

Adrian Hunsberger of the Miami-Dade extension office classifies podocarpus as very wind-tolerant (25). Don Wacker, living on a barrier island off Vero Beach that received some of the worst winds from Frances (cat 2) and Jeanne (cat 3) reported that his podocarpus "were pushed over and stripped somewhat of the top needles. They recovered after staking" (50). Larry Williams reported that podocarpus did well in Ivan (125 mph), with only minor branches splitting out (53). I heard of a few falling in Wellington (70 mph winds) but I still give this tree a **high wind tolerance**. Photo by Gene Joyner.

Powderpuff, Dwarf *(Calliandra haematocephala 'Nana'):* Zones 10 to 11. I only have two reports on this plant, so I don't know if that is enough to make an educated evaluation. However, it did great at my place (about 80 mph winds) and even more surprisingly, did well at Don Wacker's place (120 mph winds). He reported "no damage whatsoever". For more information about this plant, see "Easy Gardens for Florida".

Pongam *(Pongamia pinnata)*
This tree has a very **low tolerance for wind**.

Purple Queen *(Tradescantia pallida 'Purpurea'):* Zones 9 to 11. Several sources reported that purple queen performed badly. Since I have watched this plant handle tropical-force winds with no problem, I wonder if the water from our recent wet hurricanes caused the harm rather than the wind. Kelly Mikesell reported hers did poorly in Tampa, which had no winds over 80 mph but days of rain (35). Don Wacker from near Vero Beach, reported that his purple queen experienced 120 mph winds and had no damage (50). Do you have any more information about this plant's wind tolerance?

Red Bay *(Persea borbonia):* Zones 8 to 11.

According to Dr. Mary Duryea's survey after hurricane Andrew (145 mph), she had reports of only 10 of this species, which may not be enough for a true scientific survey. However, 80% were still standing after the storm (15). The Palm Beach Chapter of the Florida Native Plant Society had seven 'good' and five 'ok' reports on this tree's performance during Frances and Jeanne. They concluded that the tree had done well in most places. The winds in this county ranged from about 50 to 100 mph during these two storms (19). Don Wacker, living on a barrier island off Vero Beach that received some of the worst winds from

Frances (cat 2) and Jeanne (cat 3) reports that his "a very old red bay fared well during the storm and was one of the few shade trees that still had significant leaves after the storms." (50) This tree eventually reaches 40 feet in the southern area of the state, and stays smaller farther north. I have never grown this tree, but will plant one soon in my trial gardens. I have heard that it is sometimes disfigured by galls caused by insects. It has a **high wind tolerance**. Photo by Gene Joyner.

Redbud *(Cercis canadensis):* Zones 4 to 9b.

According to Teresa Watkins of Florida Yards and Neighborhoods in Orlando (about 70 mph winds), "I saw many redbuds that snapped with the summer canopy still on; our 15' specimen at our Extension office broke off to a height of three feet. This may have been due to it being planted on a corner next to the road with no wind block from any direction. Next to utility poles, it was the tallest object"(51). Larry Williams from Okaloosa County reported on redbud's performance in Ivan (125 mph winds): "A good number of redbud trees were severely damaged and either were directly taken out by Ivan or had to be removed because of extensive damage"(53). Based on these comments, redbud has a **low wind tolerance**.

Wind-Tolerance of Florida Plants

Rosewood, Indian *(Dalbergia sissoo):* These trees are brittle and have a **low wind tolerance**.

Royal Poinciana *(Delonix regia):* Zones 10 to 11.

Dan Culbert's photo of this poinciana in Vero Beach shortly after Frances and Jeanne shows that it is not very tolerant of wind. According to Dr. Mary Duryea's survey after Hurricane Andrew (145 mph), 43 % of the royal poincianas fell (15). Most people agree that this beautiful tree is quite brittle and has a **low wind tolerance**. But it has some positives aside from fact that it has been called the most beautiful tree in the world. Many of the 57% of the poincianas left after Andrew grew back with great shapes. And I found this interesting story from Ft. Myers (wind estimate 90 mph). A site where most of the golden shower trees fell (and major damage on bischoffias) reported very little damage on the royal poincianas that had been properly shaped last spring. For more information on royal poincianas, see "Easy Gardens for Florida."

Sanchezia *(Sanchezia speciosa):* Zones 10 to 11. I only had one report on this plant, which surprised me because the large leaves of the plant look like they would shred. However, this is what Don Wacker (120 mph winds) said: "No damage and was exposed to both sides of the storm." (50)

Satinleaf *(Chrysophlyllum oliveiforme):* Zones 9b to 11. The Palm Beach Chapter of the Florida Native Plant Society had five 'good' and three 'ok' reports on this tree's performance during Frances and Jeanne. The winds in the county ranged from about 50 to 100 mph during these two storms (19). According to Roger Hammer in Castellow Hammock in south Miami-Dade, none of these trees fell during hurricane Andrew. Castellow Hammock received the worst wind of the north wall of hurricane Andrew, probably more than 150 mph (22). This tree has at least a **medium wind tolerance** and probably higher.

Sausage Tree *(Kigelia pinnata):* According to Mary Duryea's survey of homeowners after hurricane Andrew (145 mph), less than 50% of these trees were left standing (15). Many of them fell in Palm Beach County with winds of 80 mph. This tree has a **low wind tolerance**.

Schefflera *(Schefflera actinophylla):* Zones 10 to 11.

This plant is considered an invasive exotic, meaning it is crowding out our natural areas. Its wood is brittle and breaks easily in the wind. But its roots are like iron, and it takes a very strong storm to uproot it. According to Dr. Mary Duryea's survey of homeowners after hurricane Andrew (145 mph), 85% of the scheffleras were left standing (15). But because of its brittle wood, this tree has a **medium wind tolerance**.

Sea Grape *(Coccoloba uvifera):* Zones 9b to 11.

Sea grapes are natives that naturally grow into multi-trunked plants, almost like huge shrubs. The sea grapes that were allowed to grow in their natural form did fairly well in the storms. However, some were trimmed into single-trunked trees, and these fell over a lot. According to Dr. Mary Duryea's survey of homeowners after hurricane Andrew (145 mph), 64% of the sea grapes were left standing. Sea grapes were one of the five species that caused the most property damage (13). Much better results were reported from the storms less than cat 5's. This plant has a **high wind tolerance** if left to grow in its natural form. This photo was taken of seagrapes 200 yards from the beach where Jeanne came ashore. They are leafing out well. The photo was taken by Daniel Culbert.

Information From Throughout the State.

Shooting Star *(Clerodendrum quadriloculare):* Zones 10 to 11. Everyone reported that the shooting stars fell apart, uprooted, defoliated, and generally did horribly in the storms. However, most of them seem to have come back, even in some of the hardest hit areas. They lost most of their leaves and branches and re-sprouted from the ground. This plant has a **low wind tolerance**.

Shrimp Plant, Golden *(Pachystachys lutea):* Zones 9 to 11.

This plant has a low tolerance for wind but did alright in very protected areas in winds of 70 mph. In more wind than that, it shredded. However, I did receive reports from areas of wind of 120 mph that it came back. Mine have recovered beautifully after a hard cut back just after the storms, three months ago, and are now blooming beautifully. This plant has a **low wind tolerance.**

Silk Oak *(Grevillea robusta):* Zones 9a to 11.

This tree is quite brittle and has a **low wind tolerance**. Photo by Stephen Brown

Spicewood *(Calyptranthus pallens):* Zones 10 to 11. The Palm Beach Chapter of the Florida Native Plant Society had all (ten) 'good' reports on this plant's performance during Frances and Jeanne. The winds in the county ranged from about 50 to 100 mph during these two storms (19). Since the reports of this group were so positive, I will plant some in my trial gardens. I still can't classify it until I get more reports. This could be a great plant for windy times!

Stopper, Redberry *(Eugenia confusa):* Zones 10 to 11.

I'm very excited about testing this plant. It is a small, slow-growing tree that eventually reaches 20 feet tall. It has the potential to reach storm superstar status. According to Dr. Mary Duryea's survey after hurricane Andrew (145 mph), she had reports on only 6 or 7 of this species, which may not be enough for a true scientific survey. However, 100% were still standing after the storm (15).The Palm Beach Chapter of the Florida Native Plant Society had six 'good' reports on this plant's performance during Frances and Jeanne. That is a perfect score for that society. The winds in the county ranged from about 50 to 100 mph during these two storms (19). This plant has at least a **high wind tolerance**. and possibly a **very high wind tolerance**. We need more data to tell. Do you have any experience with this plant in hurricanes? If so, please share it with me at colorgdn@aol.com. Photo by Joan Brookwell.

Stopper, Simpson *(Myrcianthes fragrans):* Zones 9 to 11. The Palm Beach Chapter of the Florida Native Plant Society had 16 'good' and 6 'ok' reports on this plant's performance during Frances and Jeanne. The winds in the county ranged from about 50 to 100 mph during these two storms (19). Based on this survey, this plant has at least a **medium** and probably **high wind tolerance.**

Stopper, Spanish *(Eugenia foetida):* Zones 9b to 11.

In Dr. Mary Duryea's survey of homeowners after Andrew, this tree was the top survivor, with 96% still standing after the storm (15). The Palm Beach Chapter of the Florida Native Plant Society had ten 'good' and three 'ok' reports on this plant's performance during Frances and Jeanne. The winds in the county ranged from about 50 to 100 mph during these two storms (19). I have no experience with this large shrub or small tree, but look forward to trying some in my garden. It has at least a **high wind tolerance**. This small tree grows slowly to a height of 15 to 20 feet tall.

Stopper, White *(Eugenia axillaris):* Zones 8b to 11.

According to Dr. Mary Duryea's survey after hurricane Andrew (145 mph),

Wind-Tolerance of Florida Plants

they had reports of only 10 of this species, which may not be enough for a true scientific survey. However, 100% were still standing after the storm (15). The Palm Beach Chapter of the Florida Native Plant Society had ten 'good' and one 'ok' report on this plant's performance during Frances and Jeanne. The winds in the county ranged from about 50 to 100 mph during these two storms (19). Like the redberry stopper, this tree has superstar potential except for the fact that it smells like a skunk! It is a small, slow-growing tree that eventually reaches 20 feet tall. I have never tried them, but will add some to my trial gardens shortly. This plant has at least a **high wind tolerance**.

Strangler Fig *(Ficus aurea):* Zones 9b to 11.

The Palm Beach Chapter of the Florida Native Plant Society had two good reports on this trees's performance during Frances and Jeanne. The winds in the county ranged from about 50 to 100 mph during these two storms (19). We have a large one here, and right after the storms, I thought most of it was on the ground (see photo, left, bottom) or on the roof of my son's house. Once we had a chance to clean up, I realized that the tree had simply pruned itself well. The trunk and main branches of the tree were still there, but without leaves. And my son's roof - which I had thought was quite damaged by this tree - turned out to be fine. His house was one of the few on our street without roof damage. I think the strangler fig branches actually protected his roof! And I was thrilled when I received this photo (left, top) from Randy Isler of the Sanibel-Captiva Water Department that showed a strangler fig after Charley in an area that had to have winds of at least 130 mph. The tree is standing tall and looks like it has just had a professional pruning. Except, of course, for the fact that it has no leaves. But we know how fast the leaves grow back in Florida. This tree has a **medium wind tolerance**. I would rate it higher except for the tremendous amount of debris it leaves behind in winds as low as 80 mph.

Sunshine Tree *(Erythrina variegata orientalis 'Sunshine'):* Zones 10a to 11.

The top blew off my sunshine tree with 80 mph winds. It looked like a stick after Frances. But, luckily, it's growing back quite well. For more information

on this attractive tree, see "Best Garden Color for Florida." It has a **low wind tolerance**.

Sweet Potato Vine, Tricolor *(Ipomoea batatas 'Tricolor')* Zone: used throughout Florida as an annual.

The leaves on this plant (shown above) were torn up at their home at the Breakers Resort in Palm Beach, which encountered at least 100 mph winds. But the plant grows so quickly that the new growth covered the damage in no time. This photo was taken about four weeks after Jeanne. For more information about this plant, see "Container Gardens of Florida." Sweet Potato Vines have a **medium wind tolerance**.

Sweetgum *(Liquidambar styraciflua):* Zone 8. Sweetgums are a tree of wind extremes because their crowns are easily damaged but their roots stay in the ground. So someone judging them by crown loss would classify them as having a low wind tolerance and someone judging them by their ability to keep standing would give them a high wind tolerance. Dr. Mary Duryea reports significant crown damage in Erin (85mph) and Opal (125 mph) (14). Tom MacCubbin from Orlando said that these trees are generally good survivors, but they suffer from top loss (31). Sherry Williams from Brevard County says they have a poor wind resistance, whereas the USDA lists them as very wind resistant. I would like to thank Adrian

Information From Throughout the State.

Hunsberger (13a) of Miami-Dade County Extension for summing it up well when she simply states: "The USDA list sweetgums as very wind tolerant but others consider them less tolerant because of weak crowns" (25). I am classifying this these trees as having a **medium wind tolerance**.

Sycamore *(Platanus occidentalis):* Zone 8

Dan Mullin's photo of this sycamore shows that Ivan blew the bark right off it! I received a variety of other reports on sycamores. Dr. Mary Duryea reports significant crown damage in Erin (85 mph) and Opal (125 mph) (14). Sycamores were reported uprooted or left leaning in west Volusia County where winds probably got to 60 to 70 mph. Peggy Dessaint, Manatee County Extension Agent,

reports four 40' tall sycamores with large canopies all blown over when exposed to 75 mph winds on a water-logged site (13). USDA lists these as moderately wind-resistant (25). This tree has a **medium wind tolerance.**

Tabebuia *(Tabebuia spp):* Zones 9 to 11, depending on species.

Tabebuias are one of our least-wind tolerant trees. They routinely blow down in thunder storms. I had reports from many counties where the winds can't have topped 60 mph, of lots of tabs down. All of these tabs were yellow. I don't know if the pinks did any better. If you have a tabebuia tree, consider permanent staking. Since these are small trees, they did not do too much damage, and re-establish well after they are stood up, staked, and watered in. **Low wind tolerance**. Photo by Rusty Isler.

Tallow, Chinese *(Sapium sebirerum)* This plant is invasive, meaning it crowds out our native forest. It also doesn't handle wind too well. Sherry Williams from Brevard County reported that this tree has brittle wood and is not recommended (54). Others told me it has a weak stem that snaps in half in high wind. This tree has a **low wind tolerance**.

Tamarind, Wild *(Lysiloma latisiliqua):* Zones 10 to 11. The Palm Beach

Chapter of the Florida Native Plant Society had one 'ok' and three 'so-so' reports regarding this tree's performance during Frances and Jeanne. They concluded that the tree tends to break up. The winds in the county ranged from about 50 to 100 mph during these two storms (19). **Medium wind tolerance**.

Tangerine *(Citrus reticulate):* Zones 9 to 11. According to Dr. Mary Duryea's survey of homeowners after hurricane Andrew (145 mph), 33% of these trees were left standing (14). Since this is all the information I have on this tree, I will not yet classify it's wind tolerance.

Thryallis *(Galphimia gracilis):* Zones 9 to 11.

As I explain in "Easy Gardens for Florida", this shrub is brittle. All reports showed that it broke up badly in the hurricanes but began to grow back immediately. Mine was in full flower within three months. For more information on this shrub, see "Easy Gardens for Florida." **Low wind tolerance.**

Ti Plants *(Cordyline spp):* Zones 10 to 11).

Most of them had their leaves shredded. Many fell to the ground. Most recovered with trimming and staking. For more information on this plant, see "Easy Gardens for Florida", "Best Garden Color for Florida", and "Container Gardens for Florida." **Low wind tolerance**.

Viburnum, Walters *(Viburnum obovatum):* Zones 8 to 10a. The Palm Beach Chapter of the Florida Native Plant Society had four 'good' and one 'so-so' report on this plant's performance during Frances and Jeanne. The winds in the county ranged from about 50 to 100 mph during these two storms (19). According to Theresa Watkins of Florida Yards and Neighborhoods in Orlando, "Only the top of my 15' Walters Viburnum in my yard snapped off (about two feet of it)." (51). Holly Shackelford from the Charlotte County Extension reported that this plant was "battered and leaning" from cat 4 Charley (47). This plant has a **medium wind tolerance**.

Wax Myrtle *(Myrica cerifera):* Zones 8 to 11. According to Pam Brown of the Pinellas County Extension (70-75 mph winds), the wax myrtles that were trimmed into small trees were mostly blown out of the ground throughout that county. They did not break up, but were either completely or partially out of the ground

(3). The Palm Beach Chapter of the Florida Native Plant Society had seven 'good' reports, five only 'ok' reports. four 'so-so' reports, and one person classified their wax myrtle as a 'disaster' during Frances and Jeanne. The winds in the county ranged from about 50 to 100 mph during these two storms (19). According to Sally Scalera of the Brevard County Extension: "I noticed after Charlie went through, when we drove on the beeline to Orlando, that all of the wax myrtles along the highway and around retention ponds just off the highway where blown over with the roots and soil up in the air. I now recommend that people only plant wax myrtle in protected areas since they naturally grow so thick that they can get pushed over in high winds." (44) From Peggy Dessaint, Manatee County Extension Agent, she saw two 20 foot tall plants that were fully exposed to 75 mph winds lifted right out of the ground on a water-logged site (13). Larry Williams from Okaloosa County reported on wax myrtle's performance in Ivan (125 mph): "Many wax myrtles were uprooted and injured by the storm to the point that they had to be removed. I saw whole hedges of wax myrtles that were taken out by the storm." **Low wind tolerance.**

Wild Coffee *(Psychotria spp):* Zones 8b to 11. The Palm Beach Chapter of the Florida Native Plant Society asked its members about three species of Wild Coffee. They had eleven 'good', seven 'ok' and five 'so-so' reports about these plants' performance during Frances and Jeanne. The winds in the county ranged from about 50 to 100 mph during these two storms (19). According to Mark Peters of McKee Botanical Garden in Vero Beach (120-130 mph winds), wild coffee survived five to seven days of flooding (39). **Medium wind tolerance.**

Ylang-Ylang *(Cananga odorata):* Zones 10 to 11.

The top blew off my ylang ylang tree with winds of 80 mph. It is growing back, but it looks like it might end up as a very weird tree! **Low wind tolerance**.

Yesterday, Today, and Tomorrow *(Brunfelsia grandiflora):* Zones 10 to 11.

This plant was the biggest surprise I had after my first hurricane. Previously, I had noticed a lot of problems with this plant that corresponded to times of winds in the 30 to 40 mph range and assumed it had a very low wind tolerance. I therefore expected it to be wiped out after two hurricanes and days of 80 mph winds, but that was not the case. My three plants were planted in fairly open areas and didn't even defoliate! The leaves looked good after the storms! I can only assume, therefore, that the previous problems I had with this plant were because of establishment problems and not high wind. For more information about this gorgeous plant, see "Best Garden Color for Florida." **Medium wind tolerance**.

Information From Throughout the State.

Important Points

1. Slow-growing trees are generally more wind-resistant than fast-growing trees.

2. A few trees, particularly laurel oaks, Australian pines, water oaks and *Ficus benjamina* accounted for up to 60% of the debris at polled collection sites after the hurricanes of 2004. According to Butch DuCote of FEMA, they will spend about $680 million on debris collection and removal. Based on the Santa Rosa County estimate that approximately 2/3 of their debris is vegetative, then FEMA will spend about $400 million on vegetative collection and removal. Could we save half of that by eliminating the few problem trees? How many houses would be saved from destruction by the next hurricane if we did this?

3. Many local governments require replacement of fallen trees after hurricanes, normally with large, field-grown specimen. Since many tree farms have lost their inventories after hurricanes, it makes sense to waive the size requirement. Smaller trees are much easier to find and plant, particularly for homeowners. It is also much easier to find a variety of tree species in smaller sizes, encouraging species diversification. Many of the trees we are recommending (pages 40-43) are not currently available in large quantities of field-grown sizes, but are available in smaller, containerized sizes.

Photo of Australian pines covering houses after hurricane Charley by Patrick Lynch, South Florida Water Management District.

Chapter 3
Other Reasons
Why Trees Fall

The main reason why trees fall is their wind tolerance, as discussed in the previous chapter. However, there are other environmental reasons that you should be aware of. They include the following:

1. Trees that are professionally pruned fall much less than unpruned trees.
2. Trees fall more in wet soil than in dry soil.
3. Trees fall more when planted in small spaces.
4. Trees planted close to paving fall over easier than those in open areas.
5. Trees planted too close to buildings fall over easier.
6. Trees in shallow or compacted soil blow over easier than those in soil that allow their roots to grow deeply.
7. Clumps of trees stand up better than singles
8. Recently-planted trees are more likely to fall than well-established young ones.
9. Small trees are more likely to fall than well-established, medium-sized trees.
10. Old trees blow over more than younger, well-established trees.
11. Very tall trees blow over easier than medium-sized trees.
12. Trees with defects, like rot or weak spots where the branches connect to the trunk, fall over or break up easier than strong trees.
13. Trees with two main trunks (bifurcated) split easily.
14. Trees that have had their roots cut fall over easily.
15. Look at the roots of the tree prior to planting it. If they are tightly circled around the edges, the tree is root-bound. Break up the roots with a sharp knife or machete so that they can grow outward. If not, the tree is subject to falling later.
16. Palms that have damage on their trunks from weed eaters fall over easily. (See below)

Left and above: Both of these photos show palms that had grass growing right up to their trunks. Weed eaters were used to trim the grass at the base of the trunks, and in the process, the machines cut into the trunks themselves. Breaks in the trunks of palms do not heal over, so the trunks become weak and snap at the point where the weed eater cuts. The solution to this problem is to keep grass away from tree trunks. Keep an area of at least eighteen inches of just mulch at the base of trees so that the weedeaters hit the mulch and not the tree. (Photo above: Dan Culbert. Photo opposite: Stephen Brown).

1. Trees that are professionally pruned...

This ficus tree at the Breakers Resort at Palm Beach would not be alive if it weren't trimmed before the storm. Lloyd Singleton of the Breakers had it professionally trimmed by certified arborists two days before Frances, which hit the hotel with winds of over 100 mph. The wind went through the thinned canopy instead of slamming against it and toppling the tree.

A Palm Beach County tree company told us that none of the trees it routinely trimmed went down in Jeanne or Francis. This is a staggering figure, meaning that much of the vegetative devastation could have simply been avoided!

Most of the experts I spoke with said lack of trimming was one of the major reasons why trees fell, second only to poor tree selection. Some untrimmed trees were destroyed while trimmed ones of the same type with the same amount of wind look like nothing happened.

Develop a routine tree trimming program for your garden. It is difficult to get it done at the last minute. One company told us it had 600 calls two days before one of the hurricanes hit! Obviously, they couldn't even get to a fraction of that number. And, it is dangerous to have major piles of tree clipping piled on the street before a hurricane.

fall much less than unpruned trees.

Above: Compare the two trees shown on these two pages. Can you guess which one was trimmed before hurricane Frances? Yes, the one opposite. The poor owner of the tree above is facing a bill of thousands of dollars to get this tree to the road unless he has the superhuman skill and energy to do it himself.

Officials from the Solid Waste Authority in Palm Beach County told me that they place many public service announcements with the local media about the need to trim your trees before the storms come. Well, most of us haven't been listening. But with four hurricanes hitting Florida the same year, let's hope more people get the message. There's nothing like having a tree come through your roof to get the point to sink in.

Get to know your local, top quality tree trimming company. Or learn a lot about how to safely do it yourself.

10 Tips for proper tree pruning...

Proper pruning is essential in developing a tree with a strong structure. Trees that receive the appropriate pruning measures while they are young will need less corrective pruning when they mature.

1. Identify your tree. Get a picture of the tree's natural shape and find out its normal size. Imagine how you would like your tree to look.
2. Use the proper equipment for trimming. You will need sharp tools: hand pruning shears, lopping shears and a pruning saw. Never use hedge shears to prune a tree.
3. Prune dead and broken branches back to within fi inch of the live area.
4. Go to the center of the tree and trim out small branches that are not getting enough sun.
5. Cut out the worst branches that are growing towards the center of the tree. Remove those that are growing downward and touching the ground.
6. Take out crossing, rubbing branches, leaving the healthiest one.
7. Examine young tree for dual leaders, i.e. two main trunks. Trim back one of the leaders (as long as it is 6" diameter or less). Allow one dominant leader to remain.
8. Take off suckers. These are skinny branches coming from the base and lower trunk.
9. Fix trees slowly over a 3 to 5 year period.
10. Refer to the "Trimming" notation for each plant listed in "Easy Gardens for South Florida" and "Best Garden Color for Florida". Review Easy Garden Maintenance-Trimming in the last chapter of "Easy Gardens for Florida".

Remember that the only real mistake is not to prune at all!

NOTE: Each county in Florida has pruning codes which the homeowner may wish to review.

Some of this information came from these Web sites. For more information, check them out.

International Society of Arboriculture web site:
www.treesaregood.com/treecare/pruning_young.asp

Plant Amnesty Pruning Guide: Central Florida web site:
www.plantamnesty.org/pruning_guides/pg_central_florida.htm

Fairchild Tropical Botanic Garden web site:
www.fairchildgarden.org/horticulture/n_pruning.html

And finding a good, qualified arborist.

How to Choose a Tree Service

Why hire a tree service? Proper tree care is an investment that can lead to substantial returns. Well cared-for trees are attractive and can add considerable value to your property. Poorly maintained trees can be a significant liability.

1. Call your County Extension Service and ask for three recommendations.
2. Strongly consider using a certified arborist. Florida certified arborists are individuals who have achieved a level of knowledge in the art of tree care through experience passing a comprehensive examination developed by some leading experts on tree care in Florida. They must also continue their education to maintain their certification. However, remember that certification does not guarantee quality performance - hence local references are needed.
3. Check the Yellow Pages under 'Tree Trimming' and look for ads that show the company to be a member of the National Arborist Association and states that they are certified arborists. If not stated in ad, ask them for above information.
4. Go online to the Internet and check the following sites: International Society of Arboriculture, www.ISA-arbor.com, click on link "Find an Arborist" and put in your zip code; American Society of Consulting Arborists, www.asca-consultants.org, or e mail to asca@mgmtsol.com. NOTE: Membership in professional organizations demonstrates a willingness on the part of the arborist to stay up-to-date on techniques and information.
5. Make sure they are licensed and insured for personal and property damage and worker's compensation.
6. Get references from the companies and check with your city arborist.
7. Get more than one estimate. Don't always accept the lowest bid and get your bids in writing.
8. Just because your homeowners association or your neighbors have used one particular service, do not assume that they are certified arborists.
9. Be an informed consumer. The International Society of Arboriculture offers several brochures on basic principles of tree care. For plant trimming instructions see the last chapter in "Easy Gardens for Florida". For trimming instructions on specific plants including trees, see individual plant pages in the above book and also in "Best Garden Color for Florida". County Extension Services may have instructions as well.

Some of the information obtained from the International Society of Arboriculture web site: www.treesaregood.com/treecare/hire_ arborist.asp

2. Trees fall more in wet soil than in dry soil.

Right: *This house is in Loxahatchee, about 30 miles west of the landfall of Frances and Jeanne. The winds in that location were not enough to snap or blow down this slash pine. However, the wet soil combined with the wind caused the tree to fall. Unfortunately, it punctured the roof and caused major damage to the house. Photo by Cindy Corum.*

Below: *This lot was flooded and the Norfolk Island pine, which doesn't tolerate much flooding, fell on the trailer. The bald cypress trees on the other side were not bothered by the water. Photo by Dan Culbert.*

Solutions for wet areas:

1. Fix the drainage problem. If you can't work out the problem yourself, call in a civil engineer for a consultation. Most of them work by the hour and will come to your home for a one-hour minimum. I struggled through my first drainage problem myself, wasting a lot of time, effort, and money on things that didn't work. Since then, I have called in a civil engineer several times with very satisfactory results. They figure out a solution in about fifteen minutes that would take me years of trial and error.

2. If you can't fix the underlying problem to get the area to drain properly, consider planting bald cypress, as shown in the photo at the bottom of the opposite page.

3. Sometimes there is nothing you can do. If you get record-breaking rains, like much of Florida did in 2004, your entire neighborhood may be flooded. Luckily, most of the houses in Florida are built high so the water won't ruin your home.

Above: Drainage swales are designed to hold and carry water. They are risky locations for many trees. Photo by Joleen King.

Other reasons Why Trees Fall

3. Trees planted in small spaces blow over easier.

This tree didn't have room for its roots to spread so that it would be well-anchored in its spot. Sabal palms would be the ideal choice for this spot if wind were the only consideration. But the shade would be sacrificed! Sometimes, it is worth the risk of planting a tree in a risky spot. The gains override the risks. Photo by Linda Seals of Mounts Botanical Garden, West Palm Beach.

4. Trees planted close to paving fall over easier than those planted in larger spaces where their roots have more room to spread.

Letha Giacinti, who works at the Lee County Extension, didn't expect her sycamore tree to come crashing down at her east Ft. Myers home during hurricane Charley because the winds in her area only reached about 60 or 70 mph. But its proximity to her driveway caused the roots to be stunted on that side, so that the tree didn't have the necessary stability to ride out the storm. Photo by Stephen Brown.

5. Trees planted too close to buildings fall over easier.

This is tricky, because in the next chapter, you will learn that some experts say that houses situated in the middle of wind-tolerant trees show less damage in hurricanes than houses that are open to the wind. And here I'm telling you that trees planted too close to buildings fall easily. The key is the proper distance from the building. If large trees whose roots need room to spread are planted too close to a building, it has the same effect as being near pavement - the roots don't have enough room to stabilize the tree. See the next chapter for more specifics. Photo courtesy of Leu Gardens in Orlando.

6. Trees in shallow or compacted soil blow over easier.

This makes sense. If big trees cannot put down deep roots, they will fall over easier. This is a hard situation that needs a solution. Some new home communities use shell rock for topsoil. Shell rock is what many roads are made of - it's quite hard. After the builder unloads the shell rock soil, he uses a steam roller to level it. It then resembles concrete. If you blast a big hole through it to plant your tree, the roots of the tree will probably eventually reach the edge of your hole. It might be time to consider a move. Photo by Dan Mullins.

Other reasons Why Trees Fall

7. Single trees fall easier than clumps of trees.

This concept is important to understand, because in the next chapter you will learn how to design your garden to minimize wind damage. One of the key concepts is planting trees in clumps instead of all by themselves. It makes sense that the trees inside the clumps are more sheltered than the ones at the edges. And, somehow, the whole mass holds up better than a single tree. Look how this single specimen (pictured) was so exposed to the wind that it fell over on the house. Photo by Randy Isler.

8. Recently-planted trees are more likely to fall than well-established young ones.

When the young ones fall, like this one, they can be easily uprighted provided you have the necessary manpower or equipment on hand to do it. If not, cover the roots with something that will hydrate and shade them - like wet burlap - until help has arrived. Photo by Linda Seals of Mounts Botanical Gardens in West Palm Beach.

9. Many types of small trees are more likely to fall than medium-sized trees.

Many small trees, like hibiscus and bougainvillea, topple easily during their entire lifespan. They are not supposed to grow as trees, anyway, but like vines or shrubs. Others. like the *Senna surattensis* shown at right after Charley, simply have weak roots as compared with other small trees like lignum vitae. I keep any small trees that fall easily permanently staked. If the winds are high enough, the stakes will blow down with the tree, but many staking systems keep small trees up in at least cat 1 hurricanes. See the last chapter for instructions on tree staking small trees. This photo is by Stephen Brown.

10. Old trees fall over easier than young trees in their prime.

Like people, trees have lifespans. And as they get quite old, they lose their strength. For trees that are close to buildings, I recommend check ups every few years by a certified arborist. If they are so old that they are considered hazards, they should be removed. Photo courtesy of Leu Gardens in Orlando.

11. Very tall trees fall over easier than medium-sized trees.

Trees over 40 feet tall fell more than trees that were shorter than that. For example, although royal palms (shown) don't normally fall in winds of under cat 5 force, the taller ones fall easier. According to Dr. Mary Duryea in her study after Hurricane Andrew, the average height of a fallen royal was about 45 feet while the average height of a standing royal was about 30 feet (15). Both Washingtonia and Chinese fan palms also fall easier when they are quite tall. Photo by Rusty Isler.

12. Trees with structural defects, like rot or weak spots where the branches connect to the trunk, fall over or break up easier than healthier trees.

Inspect your trees at least once a year to see if there are any visible defects on the trunks that could cause the tree to fall. If you have any doubts, call a certified arborist for his or her opinion. The photos to the right show damage to the trunk (experts call this a bark incursion) that could lead to a structural weakness that would cause the trunk to snap from even low winds. Photo at right by Dan Mullins.

13. Trees with two main trunks (bifurcated) split easily.

If you have trees with two main trunks, have an arborist take a look at them to let you know if they are hazards. They are easily split in hurricanes. Frances got the better of this one. Photo by Linda Seals of Mounts Botanical Gardens, West Palm Beach.

14. Trees that have had their roots cut fall over easily.

Roots that obviously run under sidewalks and driveways are great targets for cutting. I have done it myself, thinking that I might stop the damage to the concrete with one little cut. But by cutting a root, you also undermine the stability of the tree. Sometimes it's worth it, like if you have just spent a fortune on gorgeous old Chicago brick pathways. You can do this as long as you understand the risks - that the entire tree might come down as the result of a few quick root removals. Photo by Dan Mullins.

Chapter 3

Designing to Minimize
Wind Damage

After the hu

This is my winter garden, which I could hardly recognize after Frances and Jeanne. This garden is next to a pond and wide open to the wind. It was also planted with plants that don't take wind well, like cassia trees, angelwing begonias, and ti plants.

My pool garden is on the next two pages, and the difference between the two gardens inspired me to write this book. The plants looked untouched after two hurricanes. The garden is protected by a fence and wind-tolerant palms. Most of the shrubs and groundcovers are also wind-tolerant. Turn the page and take a peek.

I am restoring my winter garden much as it was. The purpose of the garden is to display the best of our winter flowering plants... and it will stay that way. Only about five large plants died. The rest recovered after cutbacks and fertilization.

I'm not recommending that people who love plants should restrict themselves to only wind-tolerant species. That would take the joy and discovery out of gardening for us.

However, it is so nice to have one garden on my property that looks good when everything else looks so depressing! And I am happy to pass on my tips for garden protection. Maybe you'll get some ideas that will bring you joy instead of heartache after our next storm.

Before the hurricanes

This garden inspired me to write this book. It was the only part of my property that wasn't devastated by Frances and Jeanne (thirty miles southeast of the eyes of both). After we cleaned the pool and picked up some debris, it looked just like it had before the storm! Even the containers (we didn't have time to move them before the storm) looked great! The garden is protected by a six-foot wooden fence and a double layer of moderately wind-tolerant palms. A path runs between the two rows of palms, connecting the brick deck with the raised pavilion. See the next two pages for descriptions of the plants that were used.

has no storm damage...why?

After the hurricanes

Palms used as barriers to protect...

Foxtail Palms   **Coconut Palms**   **Palmettos**

Christmas Palms   **Thatch Palms**   **Pygmy Date Palms**

wind-tolerant shrubs and groundcovers

These palms (left) provided a wind screen for the garden on the previous two pages. On the whole, palms are more wind-tolerant than trees with leaves. They also don't drop as many leaves and branches during a storm. All of these species are rated as "high" for wind tolerance in my "Easy Gardens for Florida" book. The foxtail palm is rated medium. The hurricanes of 2004 were the first storms after foxtail palms were widely planted. We were quite pleased with their strength. They held up considerably better than royal palms. However, for my friends in zone 9, only the palmettos and pygmy date palms are tolerant of hard freezes.

The shrubs and groundcovers (right) did very well. I didn't even have to cut any of them back after the storm. With all the rest of my gardens devastated, it was wonderful to have one spot that looked good. All of these plants are rated medium or high wind tolerance except the dwarf chenille. It had been untested for wind tolerance prior to the 2004 storms, but now we know! However, hurricane winds diminish as you get closer to the ground, so groundcovers always do better than trees.

Remember the importance of knowing more than just the wind tolerance of a plant before buying it. See "Easy Gardens for Florida" or "Best Garden Color for Florida" for complete plant profiles on these plants.

Bulbine

Croton

Dwarf Chenille

Aechmea Bromeliad

Purple Queen

Dracaena Reflexa

Ideas to protect your garden from wind...

*Both "Easy Gardens for Florida" and "Best Garden Color for Florida"
have chapters on salt and wind. Check them out for additional ideas about
designing to minimize wind damage.*

Before

After

**Create a sabal palm forest to
protect the plants underneath.**
Sabal palms are one of the
most wind-tolerant trees in
Florida. But not the most
attractive! They do not look
great as a front yard specimen
tree (above). Use them as
nature does, in informal
forests. Plant them close
together to protect delicate
plants underneath. See more
about this project in *Easy
Gardens for Florida,* Chapter
13, "Garden Style."

Before

After

Use wind-tolerant trees to create a wind screen. This house is close to the ocean and the wind was ruining the garden. Palms were planted into the hedge to form a wind break. It worked well, but would have been better had there been enough room to plant clumps of trees rather than a single row. See more about this project in *Easy Gardens for Florida,* Chapter 11, "Easy Gardens for Salt and Wind."

Some astounding findings from Charley

This page: This house was wide open to the wind and badly damaged. Photo by Randy Isler.

Dr. Robert Loflin is the natural resources director for the city of Sanibel. He told me that when he and the emergency teams entered the island after Charley had devastated it, they noticed an unforeseen trend. The houses with no vegetation and the houses with tall, wind-sensitive trees were damaged more than the houses surrounded by wind-tolerant trees. He wrote about it in a letter to the editor of *Wildland Weeds:* "As far as hurricane effects on trees go, it was abundantly clear that properties well vegetated with 20'-40' trees of either native or exotic variety fared far better in terms of structural wind damage than those with grassy lawns, on golf courses, or with tall exotic trees" (29).

This page: Rusty Isler's house on Ft. Myers Beach was not damaged as much as other nearby homes that were wide-open to the wind. His live oaks are recovering well. Photos by Rusty Isler.

Rusty Isler, who took many of the photos for this book, agrees with Dr. Loflin. He works for the Island Water Association which provides the water service for Sanibel and Captiva. Rusty was very involved in repairing water lines after Charley and saw a lot of damage.

His home on neighboring Ft. Myers Beach is in a wooded location. Although the winds weren't as bad as on Sanibel and Captiva, his home fared better than his neighbors who had more open landscapes.

Important Wind Screen Guidelines

1. Plant clumps of trees rather than singles. Clumps, which hold up better in wind, should contain at least five trees.

2. Don't plant so close to the house that the plants touch the walls or you may create a highway for insects to enter your home.

3. Keep the larger trees a distance from your house. If the roots are too close, the tree loses some of its stability. And, remember, <u>do not plant trees that grow over 40 feet tall within falling distance of your home.</u>

4. If possible, keep your front door visible from the street. You'll have less break-ins that way.

5. If your neighborhood regulations limit the amount of planting you can do in front, concentrate on the sides and back. At least you'll have three sides protected.

6. Use the most wind-tolerant material on the outer edge of your screen (see pages 40-43). This is the area that will receive the most wind. Plant more delicate material between the wind screen and the house.

7. Understand your risk. Hurricanes are never predictable, and any tree can fall with enough wind. Tornados can easily down wind-tolerant trees in a cat 1 hurricane. And there are experts who recommend no trees within falling distance of the house.

8. Study Chapter 3, so you don't plant trees in areas where they are likely to fall.

These photos show protected landscapes designed by Bill Reeve and Jennifer Atwood of Botanical Visions in Boca Raton (phone: 561-361-6677).

Protect your home with wind tolerant trees...

This page and opposite, top: This backyard was designed by Bill Reeve and Jennifer Atwood from Botanical Visions in Boca Raton (phone, 561-361-6677) to create a private oasis of tranquility for the owners. An added benefit of the wooded setting is that it acts as a wind screen for the house. Be sure and use wind-tolerant plants for your wind screen, like the ones shown on pages 40-43. If you plant weak plants in this kind of arrangement, it can backfire and fall on your home instead of protecting it. **Opposite, bottom:** This home was built in a natural wooded setting, featuring lots of wind-tolerant live oaks and sabal palms, which shelter it from the elements. The oak is too close to the brick path, however.

that don't grow more than 40 feet tall.

Placing trees: Plant small trees under power lines.

Extended time periods without electricity was the hardest part of the storm for many people. If power lines are constructed near natural forests, it is understandable that the forests not be removed. However, it makes no sense to plant trees near power lines that will eventually grow into them. Imagine what it costs to run all those trucks shown to the right! The face of Jackson Mullins (opposite, bottom) reflects that sadness and frustration of many Floridians who experienced extended power outages. Jackson's dad, Dan Mullins, took both the photo below and the photo of Jackson. Jackson took the photo of the trucks. Do we have a budding photographer here?

FPL recommends the following setbacks for trees from power lines:

Large Trees: 30 feet

Medium Trees: 20 feet

Small trees: May be planted adjacent to power lines.

Chapter 5
Storm Preparation
& Aftercare

1. Preparation

2. Don't get overwhelmed.

3. Be careful.

4. After the storm, First priority: Upright your trees.

5. Check roots of plants that are still standing.

6. Test your plants to see which are dead and which are alive.

7. Water any plants damaged by salt water.

8. Trim any shrubs and groundcovers that look bad.

9. Fertilize carefully.

10. Move shade plants that are getting too much sun.

11. Remove any dangling branches.

12. Take care of your palms.

13. Watch out for old world climbing fern.

14. Care for your damaged trees.

15. Remove any dangerous trees.

These photos were taken at Heathcote Botanical Gardens by Sam and Allie Comer. Heathcote is located in Ft. Pierce, which received the worst of Frances and Jeanne.

1. Preparation

Routine Maintenance

Gardens that are well-maintained throughout the year do much better in hurricanes than those that are neglected. We spent 10 years testing and researching maintenance practices for our "Easy Gardens for Florida" book and suggest you do the following:

1. Read Chapter 8 which will teach you to properly water your garden. The most common mistake made in Florida gardens is over-watering.
2. Read Chapter 14 which will teach you to properly mulch, trim, and fertilize your garden. And to make shopping easy, take the book with you when you shop for mulch or fertilizer so that you can be sure of purchasing the right products. This chapter teaches you how to maintain effectively with the least amount of time possible.

Tree Trimming

Set up a program for annual tree trimming, either done by yourself or a professional company. This can do more than any other maintenance chore to save your garden. See pages 96-97 for guidelines. Be sure that your trimming is done well before the storm, in time for the debris to be gone from the curb. Trimming should be routine, not a last minute chore.

Supplies to Have on Hand to Help your Garden Recuperate

Be sure you have these supplies before the storm. They may be extremely difficult to find after it's over. This list is not all that you need, just things for the garden. Read your local papers or watch the local tv to see other products, like batteries and radios, that you will need. I never saw a list of garden products before the storm, and it made it quite difficult afterwards.

1. Generator, the largest you can afford. Be sure to maintain it regularly. We had two generators before Frances and thought we were well-prepared. Neither of them worked, ever, even after attempting to have them repaired. One of them had never been turned on! They need to be turned on and regularly maintained, like a car. Follow the instructions from the manual.

When you are sizing your generator, try to get one large enough to run your sprinkler pump if you have automatic sprinklers. Although most hurricanes bring a lot of rain, it is often hot and dry for weeks afterwards, and your garden may need water before the power comes back on.

Generators have electrical outlets in them. You can plug in whatever you like. It is much easier to have an electrician wire your house so that you can use one plug to turn on however much the generator can handle. Compare this with running 15 or 20 extension cords and it's definitely worth the extra money. Remember that being without electricity is often the hardest part of the storm, often lasting for weeks. The more preparation you do ahead of time, the easier it will be on you and your family.

Follow all the safety rules in the manual. Every time there is a hurricane, someone dies because they run the generator indoors, or in the garage. The carbon monoxide fumes kill them.

2. Hose and Manual Sprinklers

You will need a hose immediately after the storm, so be sure you have it on hand. A manual sprinkler also comes in handy to water if your power is not yet restored to run your automatic system.

3. Stakes and soft rope

Count on your small trees being down and in need of stakes. It is important that you get this done as soon as possible, and it might be impossible to buy them after the storms.

4. Rakes, shovels, wheelbarrows, and hand clippers for after storm clean-up

5. Chain saw and safety instructions for the saw. Many accidents after storms are related to chain saws. Follow the manufacturer's instructions and go to http://muextension.missouri.edu.explore.agguides/agengin/go1959.html for safety instructions. Do this now, while you have power for your computer.

6. Ladder and ladder safety instructions from http://www.pp.okstate.edu/ehs/links/ladder.html. You may need a ladder to climb on your roof after the storm.

Move or Tie Down Anything that Could Blow Away

Your tv and newspapers will be loaded with instructions of what to bring inside before the storm. Here are some things they didn't tell me:

1. Lay down arches if they are not well-anchored into the ground. The vines that are growing on them will do much better on the ground where the wind is minimal.

*Above, left: Carol Hall from Palm Beach Gardens came up with the idea of using bungee cords to stabilize her fountain. **Right:** Cindy Corum from Loxahatchee left her arch standing, as I did, before Frances. The vine took quite a beating before it fell. Better to lay it down before the storm.*

2. After the storm: Go easy on yourself!

Above: *Many of the plants in my nursery were crushed by falling branches, or whole downed trees. If you look closely, you can see that shrimp plants in nursery pots are under this mess. They were neatly lined up in rows before the hurricanes.*

We evacuated for hurricane Frances. When I heard that it was only a cat 2 and that the eye hit thirty miles northeast of my property, I didn't think we had been hit too hard.

Then I got home. My property, which is an important part of my soul, was devastated. I'll always remember that first walk through my eight acres. I left my car in the street because the driveway was filled with trees. It was so bad that it seemed unreal, like a nightmare.

My little nursery was trashed. The plants were all either crushed by trees or under water. And my trial gardens, those spots that I had nurtured for nine years and spent most of my days either looking at or working near, were a disaster.

Many small trees were down that I knew we could save if we only had stakes. We used eight-foot landscape timbers for stakes, which are hard for me to handle. All I had to do was call the local home improvement store and ask them to deliver some. I picked up my

cell phone (the regular phones were out) and couldn't get a signal. The tower was down. So I drove to the nearest home improvement store, which was tricky because the street lights were out and power lines were littering the streets.

When I reached the home improvement store, there were hundreds of people in line. The power was out so the staff was taking the customers through one by one with flashlights. It looked like I would have to spend the night at the store before getting my stakes, so I

Above: The plants in my small nursery that weren't completely crushed died from flooding. We had 31 inches of rain in a month.

left, deciding to drive until I could get my cell phone to work. I drove about twenty miles (with great difficulty, I might add) and finally got a cell phone signal. I called five home improvement stores, and none of them had phones working.

Then, I drove from one home improvement store to another, looking for one that had power. Finally, I found one, and entered triumphantly to score twenty-four landscape timbers. I found a large cart, found the timbers, and lifted the first one onto the cart. It was hard. I

realized that I couldn't physically handle them, and the store had no one who could help me. I left with only one, feeling completely overwhelmed and depressed.

I had spent an entire day looking for twenty-four landscape timbers and came home with one. I was unbelievably stressed, having no idea how we were going to make any progress if I could only do so little in a day.

I also had the terrifying experience of running into a hang-

ing power line with my car. It was hanging over the road, still attached to leaning poles on either side. For a moment, I thought it would behead me, but I slammed on my brakes before it hit the car. A man was not so lucky the next day, and was electrocuted by such an encounter.

Another hurricane hit us a few weeks later. At that point, I was numb. Nothing else could bother me.

Local hospitals were reporting a record number of stress-related illnesses. We called it storm stress.

Three months have passed. The nursery has been cleaned up and most of the insurance payments received. The gardens are looking much better. We've been planting lots of annual flowers, which really cheer us up.

We still have about four acres to clean. These are areas that we don't have to look at every day, so we're not too rushed to finish it.

Hurricanes are very difficult times for anyone who gets hit. Now that I've been through my first two, I won't be in such a hurry to clean up next time. I'll take it easier, maybe even leaving the area until power is restored. Those first few days after the storm are not the time to attempt to get a lot done!

You'll be surprised how fast...

Right after Frances

Right after Frances

When I saw my garden after the storm, I was upset and overwhelmed. I thought it would take years to get it back in shape. My husband kept bemoaning the fact that we had no flowers. I would have felt much better had I known that it would only take a few months to clean up and replant. I'm so happy and appreciative now when I look out at all the flowers!

your garden recovers!

Three months later

3. Be Careful!

More people are killed accidentally after hurricanes than during the storm. Be careful, even more careful than you would be doing the same chores at other times. Storm stress makes you much more vulnerable to accidents than at normal times.

You may be doing things that you have no experience with, like operating chain saws and climbing all over roofs. If you are scared in the least of any chore, don't do it. Your concentration may be numbed by storm stress, and getting something done is not worth breaking a leg or worse. It doesn't make much sense to do all you do before a storm to protect yourself and your home and then break your neck falling off a ladder the day after the storm!

Learn to ask for help. Friends and neighbors are very willing to help in times of disaster.

Chain saws and ladders are very dangerous. See page 125 for Web sites to visit now, before you have no power, to learn about chain saw and ladder safety. It is so upsetting to see news stories about people who die from accidents after hurricanes. Do your part to keep this from happening to you.

Left: *Workers at Heathcote Botanical Garden are using two of the most dangerous tools for after-storm accidents, ladders and chain saws. Photo by Sam and Allie Comer at Heathcote Botanical Garden in Ft. Pierce.*

Above: *Downed power lines can kill. Stay away from them, and call the power company whenever you see some that could endanger people. Even though the power company is busy after the storm, they prioritize repairing dangerous lines. Photo by Rusty Isler.*

Right: *Be especially careful with chain saws. They can easily cause serious injury. Photo by Carol Hall.*

Can you see these power lines?

The scariest thing that happened to me after Frances and then again after Jeanne was hitting power lines with my car. Some of them are hanging low across the road, as shown in this photo. I didn't see them until they were already across my windshield. Luckily, I was able to slam on my brakes before I either broke the line or it went through my windshield. A man was killed in Palm Beach County in just such an accident after Frances. If you see a situation like this, call the power company immediately and very clearly tell them about a very dangerous situation. Photo by Rusty Isler.

Right, top: This Australian pine is a hazard to anyone passing under it.

Right, Bottom: Can you see the power lines running through this fallen ficus? Remember to be very conscious of power lines when removing any vegetation. Both photos on this page by Rusty Isler.

3. First priority: Upright any trees you can

Above: *One of the biggest mistakes made after hurricanes is neglecting downed trees that could be saved. If a road needs to be cleared of trees so that traffic can pass, the crew can simply put trees that fit on the side of the road, place wet burlap on the roots, and come back when there is more time to replant the trees. Photo by Linda Seals, Mounts Botanical Garden in West Palm Beach.*

Left: *Often, downed trees are too large to upright without equipment. If you have to wait for help, put burlap or soil on the roots to keep them damp until help arrives. Photo taken by Sam and Allie Comer at Heathcote Botanical Gardens in Ft. Pierce.*

Right, top: *This tabebuia tree is a valuable specimen worth thousands. It is definitely worth some extra effort to save it. Photo by Linda Seals.*

Right, bottom: *This tree was photographed six weeks after Jeanne. The lawn service could have uprighted it in about five minutes!*

Staking small trees is **quite easy.**

Left: *We use 8 foot landscape timbers for stakes. We bury them 3 to 4 feet in the ground. The tree is tied to the stake with soft rope. Be sure to loosen the rope as the tree grows so that it doesn't strangle it. Water these trees just as you would a new one. See the "Watering" chapter in the "Easy Gardens for Florida" book.*

Below: *A lot of small trees for example Senna surattensis (shown below) are very sensitive to wind. One idea is to stake them permanently. However, you need to be careful with the staking, so it doesn't kill the tree, like the one on the opposite page. Photo by Stephen Brown.*

Opposite top: *This tree was staked and then neglected. No one checked the tie to be sure it wasn't cutting into the trunk. Photo by Stephen Brown.*

Opposite bottom: *As the tree grew, no one loosened the rope, and it strangled the tree. Photo by Stephen Brown.*

More Storm Aftercare

5. Check roots of plants that are still standing.

Many plants have lost soil around their roots. They may have blown around so much in the storm that the soil is hollowed out at their base. The roots need to be covered as soon as possible. Add soil to fill in these holes. Then alternate watering and more soil until all the air pockets are filled. You will know that the air pockets are filled because you will see no more bubbles. Push the hose down into the hole several times to fill it with water, and keep doing this until you see no bubbles. Be sure to keep the soil at its original level, not piling any up around the roots. Any soil piled up around the base of the plant higher than it was before the storm can rot the stem or trunk.

Left: Look at the roots of these two plants shortly after a hurricane. You can see that they blew around enough to expose the roots. Photo by Dan Culbert of Okeechobee.

Above: If you don't have time to find some soil, just use lawn clippings. The point is to cover the roots as soon as possible so that they don't get sunburned. Photo by Dan Cuthbert of Okeechobee.

6. Test your plants to see which are dead and which are alive.

Scratch some bark off a branch. If you see green underneath, the plant is alive. This works on shrubs and trees. Do not scratch the bark of palms because it does not grow back.

7. Water any plants damaged by salt water.

Water them with fresh water as soon as possible to wash out the salt from the soil. Afterwards, water more frequently than other plants. This is only possible if your water is functioning when you return home. In areas that are badly damaged, it could take weeks for the water system to be repaired.

More Storm Aftercare

8. Trim any shrubs and groundcovers that look bad.

Now is the time to break the trimming rules for your shrubs. If it looks bad, cut it, regardless of time of year. See the last chapter of "Easy Gardens for Florida" for general trimming instructions. See each plant profile in both "Easy Gardens for Florida" and "Best Garden Color for Florida" for trimming instructions on individual plants. Remember - pay no attention to normal trimming times. Cut back anything that looks bad except palms.

9. Fertilize carefully.

Fertilize with a mild, slow-release blend. Harsh fertilizers can hurt damaged roots. If roots are badly damaged, let the plant recover for a few months before fertilizing. For more information about what fertilizer types and methods to use, see the last chapter of "Easy Gardens for Florida."

10. Move shade plants that are getting too much sun.

Shade gardens may be exposed to too much sun if the trees that were shading them are gone or leafless. If possible, move them to areas of more shade.

11. Remove any dangerous branches.

Check your trees for branches that are dangling but still attached. These are dangerous because they could easily fall on a person.

12. Take care of your palms.

The center bud of the plant is the spike that grows out of the center. Usually, it is not so noticable as on this palm, that was damaged by the wind. The bud is the most delicate part of the palm. If it is broken, the palm may die. Treat it gently. Photo by Stephen Brown.

Be careful with the trunk on palms. If they are damaged, they do not heal. Insects and diseases can enter through the cut. Photo by Stephen Brown.

Leave the brown fronds on the tree until they fall off. The palm gets nutrients from them.

Have patience with your palms. They often take longer to heal than other types of trees. This coconut palm will probably heal itself. Photo by Stephen Brown.

13. Watch Out for Old World Climbing Fern

Old world climbing fern is an invasive exotic plant. It spreads so aggressively that it can smother whole forests. Since it is spread primarily by wind, hurricanes can increase its range. Old world climbing fern is very difficult to get rid of once it is established.

Australian pine and melaleuca are two invasive trees that are also spread by wind in the southern and south-central parts of Florida. Go to http://www.fleppc.com for the latest information regarding identification and eradication of invasive plants.

14. Care for your damaged trees.

If you have a Norfolk pine near your home, and it looks like this, have it removed. It should never have been planted so close because it could fall on the house when the next big one hits. However, if you are willing to invest a tidy sum in its renovation, it can be done. Cut the damaged branches off at the juncture with the trunk so that new branches will sprout. If you don't make the cut, no branch will grow there, and the shape of the tree will be quite peculiar. The new branches will eventually grow out, but it takes quite a while. Since it requires a cherry-picker truck to reach the taller areas of this tree, it may be cheaper to remove it. This is the only pine that regenerates branches. Photo by Stephen Brown.

Fruit trees can be crowned (removing the top) and shaped. This tree can be saved.

This black olive can be saved, but I wouldn't want one of these weak trees so close to my house. To renovate this tree, remove the branch over the red car; thin and shape the rest of the tree.

This tree can be saved, but in the long run it should be taken down because it will not do well in future hurricanes. If you want to attempt a renovation, thin out and shape the clumps.

14. Care for damaged trees.

This gumbo limbo was bent by the wind. If the tree is stable, don't straighten it because it will straighten itself over time. Straightening a tree this size would require equipment to re-plant it.

This mahogany can be shaped and laterals (side branches) thinned. But will probably break up again in heavy wind.

This ylang ylang tree should be taken down. It will never recover and look like it should.

This bifurcated tree is quite a challenge. Have an arborist look at any you have to see if they recommend removal. Photo by Linda Seals, Mounts Botanical Garden, West Palm Beach.

Hatracking, One of the most expensive.

Hatracking is illegal in most communities. When all major branches are cut, the new growth is so thick that the tree becomes a dangerous "sail" during the next storm. See pages 96 and 97 for proper tree-trimming tips.

mistakes you can make.

15. Remove **dangerous trees.**

Remove any trees that are obviously dangerous, like the pines that Dan Mullins photographed above. Consult an arborist if you're not sure if the tree is dangerous, like this queen palm. Or, better yet, remove dangerous trees before they fall on your house so that your house doesn't end up like the ones to the right (photo by Patrick Lynch, South Florida Water Management District).

What happens to all that trash...

Before

After

that seems to disappear like magic?

Left: The garbage disappeared but so did the grass, which died from having the garbage on it so long. The grass was replaced before the 'after' photo was taken. Photo by Dan Culbert.
Above: This vegetation was not piled up by man, it was left that way by Charley. Photo by Barbara Hadsell.
Right: Carol Hall took this photo of garbage in front of her house after Frances.

What happens to all that trash?

Above: Greg Cotton, supervisor of this debris site, with a pile that represents about 20% of what had been collected in two months after Ivan. Opposite: Greg Cotton standing near an incinerator pit. Both photos by Barbara Hadsell.

Barbara Hadsell helped me research this book. She went to the Panhandle to gather information on the effects of Hurricane Ivan to vegetation in Santa Rosa and surrounding counties that were devastated. The Director of Public Works, Mr. Avis Whitfield, arranged for her to visit one of 11 sites in the county where hurricane debris was being gathered, separated and "processed."

She met with **Greg Cotton, Road Inspection Supervisor, at the debris site at the Holley OLF Whiting Field, no longer used by the Navy and loaned to the Santa Rosa County Road Department for debris processing.** Mr. Cotton supervises all 11 county debris sites plus the two sites open to the public. His staff increased from 10 to 25 during the peak of debris removal and he also coordinated the efforts of up to 50 private contractors. Between 10,000 and 13,000 cubic yards a day were processed at this one site over a five to six week period. Two-thirds of the debris was vegetative. These pictures of vegetative debris represent only 20% of what had been collected by November 24 following Ivan, which made landfall in September. The rest had been burned in incinerator pits dug into the ground. Burning is accelerated and smoke is reduced by fans running on generators.

Here's one of eleven collection sites in Santa Rosa County

$30 million spent in only one county!

      This site is near a lumber yard, so a private contractor has salvaged the good trees for lumber. Debris sites in other parts of the state, where no local lumber yards exist have had to burn everything including the "good" trees that could be used for lumber.

      The measurement of the debris was done from the tower where each filled truck would stop before going to the separation area. The debris is measured so that the county knows how much to pay the contractor who brought it in. Their pay is based on the number of cubic yards of debris they bring in.

      The Grant Backhoe helped move the debris to the proper area and was brought from Chicago in 3 pieces because of its huge size. Mr. Cotton stated that to date over 3 million cubic yards of debris have been collected in Santa Rosa County, with 2 million of that being vegetative. The cost to the county will be a total of $30 million dollars--$19 million spent as of Dec. 20, 2004. If the county does not receive federal money for this expenditure, it will have to borrow the money.

      In addition to vast vegetative destruction, Hurricane Ivan totally demolished 1064 homes in Santa Rosa County. In Escambia County over 6000 homes were lost including one span of the I-10 bridge over the bay at Pensacola.

Left: *The giant backhoe that was brought from Chicago in three pieces.*
Right: *Greg Cotton standing in the tower, where the incoming debris is measured from.*
Below: *Barbara Hadsell, our researcher, standing near some wood that will be picked up by a lumber yard.*

Conclusion

Photo by Rick Joyce

I hope you've learned something that will help you during these windy times...

And lead to some wonderful, flowery days in your future!

Sources and Bibliography

1. Black, Robert J. "Caring for Hurricane-Damaged Home Landscape Plants". Fact Sheet ENH 110, A series of the Environmental Horticulture Department, Florida Cooperative Extension Service, Institute of Food and Agricultural Sciences, University of Florida, 2000.

2. Bolles, Beth, Extension agent, Horticulture specialist, Escambia County. Email correspondence. 2004.

3. Brown, Pam, Pinellas County Extension. Email correspondence. 2004.

4. Brown, Stephen H. "Palm Wind Hardiness List". Email correspondence. November, 2004.

5. Brown, Stephen H. "Salvaging Hurricane -Damaged Tropical Fruit Trees". Adapted from an email by Dr. Jonathan Crane, Tropical Research and Education Center, Homestead, Florida.

6. Burban, Lisa L. and Andresen, John W. *Storms Over the Urban Forest,* Second Edition, 1994. Chapter 8. Dempsey, Gene. "Notes from Hurricane Andrew". Cooperators: USDA Forest Service, Northeastern Area, USDA Forest Service, Southern Region, University of Illinois, Department of Forestry, Illinois Department of Conservation, Division of Forest Resources, Florida Department of Agriculture and Consumer Services, Division of Forestry. Found at http://www.na.fs.ded.us/spfo/pubs/uf/sotuf/sotuf.htm.

7. Burch, Derek. "How to Minimize Wind Damage in the South Florida Garden". Document number ENH 64, one of a series of the Department of Environmental Horticulture, Florida Cooperative Extension Service, Institute of Food and Agricultural Sciences, University of Florida, First printed September, 1985. Revised October 2003.

8. Caldwell, Doug. "Proper Pruning Reduces Storm Damage". Collier County Horticulture. University of Florida, IFAS Extension. http://collier.ifas.ulf.edu.

9. Conner, William H. "Impact of Hurricanes on Forests of the Atlantic and Gulf Coasts". Reprinted with permission from Aimlee D. Laderman, Editor, Swamp Research Center, PO Box 689, Woods Hole, MA 02543. Accepted for publication in *Coastally Restricted Forests,* Oxford University Press.

10. Crane, J.H., Balerdi, Carlos F. "Effect of Hurricane Andrew of Mango Trees in Florida and Their Recovery". ISHS Acta Horticulturae 455; V International Mango Symposium. Found at http://www.actahort.org/books/455/455_42.html.

11. Culbert, Daniel. Okeechobee County Extension Service. Email correspondence.

12. Dawson, Jackie. Email correspondence

13. Dessaint, Peggy, Extension Agent, Commercial Landscape Horticulture, University of Florida Extension/IFAS, Manatee County. Email correspondence. 2004.

14. Duryea, Mary L."Wind and Trees: Surveys of Tree Damage in the Florida Panhandle after Hurricanes Erin and Opal". Circular 1183, one of a series of the School of Forest resources and Conservation, Florida Cooperative Extension Service, Institute of Food and Agricultural Sciences, University of Florida, 1997.

15. Duryea, Mary L., Blakeslee, George M., Hubbard, William G., and Vasquez, Ricardo A. "Wind and Trees; A Survey of Homeowners after Hurricane Andrew". Journal Series R-04822 of the Institute of Food and Agricultural Sciences, University of Florida, Gainesville, Florida 32611.

16. Duryea, Mary L., Assistant Dean for Research and Assistant Director, IFAS, University of Florida. Email and phone correspondence.

17. Florida Gardening Forum, *Garden Web.* http://forums.gardenweb.com/load/flgard/msg100117116999.html

18. FloridaGardener.com. "Hurricane Resistant Trees for Your Landscape." 2004.

19. Florida Native Plant Society, Palm Beach County Chapter. Results of a survey of the membership shortly after Frances and Jeanne hit Palm Beach County. The survey was conducted informally. The main purpose of the survey was to lead a discussion at the October 2004 meeting. They collected about 40 surveys. This was not a thorough data collection effort and should not be considered as such. Also, information was not collected on non-native plants for comparison.

20. Gilman, Edward F. "What we Leaned from Recent Hurricanes and Tropical Storms". 2004

21. Gilman, Edward F. "Evaluating and Treating Landscape Trees Following a Hurricane". Fact Sheet ENH 105, one in a series of the Environmental Horticulture Department, Florida Cooperative Extension Service, Institute of Food and Agricultural Sciences, University of Florida, 2000.

22. Hammer, Roger. Naturalist and director of Castellow Hammock Nature Center for the Miami-Dade Parks Department. Phone and email correspondence.

23. Heathcote Botanical Gardens, Ft. Pierce

24. Hightower, Cliff. "Study Focuses on Wind Resistant Trees". *Hernando Today, Online Edition.* November 9, 2004.

25. Hunsberger, Adrian, M.S. Urban Horticulture Agent, Entomologist, Master Gardener Coordinator, University of Florida/IFAS, Miami-Dade County Extension.

26. "Hurricanes Charley, Frances and Jeanne: Their Effects on Brevard County's Landscape".

27. Jarrell, Jerry D. (retired), Mayfield, Max, Rappaport, Edward N, NOAA/NWS/Tropical Prediction Center, Miami, FL and Landsea, Christopher, NOAA/AOML/Hurricane Research Division, Miami, FL. "The Deadliest, Costliest, and Most Intense United States Hurricanes from 1900 to 2000 (and Other Frequently Requested Hurricane Facts). Found at http://www.nhc.noaa.gov/pastdec.shtml.

28. Leu Botanical Gardens, Orlando

29. Loflin, Robert K, Ph.D., Letter to the editor, "The Agony that has been the History of Australian Pines on Public Lands on Sanibel Island is all but Over". *Wildland Weeds.* Florida Exotic Pest Plant Council and the Southeast Exotic Pest Plant Council. Gainesville, FL. Winter, 2004.

30. Lovelace, John K. and McPherson, Benjamin F. "Effects of Hurricane Andrew (1992) on Wetlands in Southern Florida and Louisiana". From the "National Water Summary on Wetland Resources". United States Geological Survey Water Supply Paper 2425.

31. MacCubbin, Tom, University of Florida, IFAS, Extension Agent IV for Orange County, Florida. Email correspondence.

32. Martin, Carol, and Wacker, Don. Email correspondence. Their home on a barrier island near Vero Beach is about two blocks from the ocean and one lot off the intracoastal/Indian River. This area was just north of the eyewall of both Jeanne and Frances, and had some of the strongest winds (120 mph) of those storms. They also had a tornado and 31 inches of rain in 33 days.

33. McKee Botanical Garden, Vero Beach.

34. Meerow, Alan W. "Salvaging Hurricane-Damaged Palms in the Nursery". Fact Sheet ENH 106, a series of the Environmental Horticulture Department, Cooperative Extension Service, Institute of Food and Agricultural Sciences, University of Florida. 2000.

35. Mikesell, Kelly. Email correspondence.

36. Moor, Louise. Email correspondence.

37. Mounts Botanical Garden, West Palm Beach, FL.

38. Mullins, Dan. Phone conversation. County Agent, UF/IFAS Santa Rosa County Extension.

39. Peters, Mark. Director of Horticulture, McKee Botanical Garden, Vero Beach. Email correspondence.

40. Pielke, Roger A. Jr. Simonpietri, Chantal. Oxelson, Jennifer. "Thirty Years After Hurricane Camille: Lessons Learned, Lessons Lost". *Hurricane Camille Project Report.* Found at http://sciencepolicy.colorado.edu/home-pages/roger_pielke/camille/report.html.

41. Price, Terry. "Storm Damage". *Forest Health Guide for Georgia Foresters.* Georgia Forestry Commission. Fall 2001.

42. Scalera, Sally. "Hurricane a Harsh Reminder to Landscape Carefully".

43. Scalera, Sally. "Choose Wisely When you're Replanting Trees". Saturday, October 16, 2004.

44. Scalera, Sally. Email correspondence, 2004.

45. Seals, Linda. Phone correspondence. University of Florida Master Gardener Program, Mounts Botanical Garden, West Palm Beach, Florida.

46. Seme, Sheila. Email correspondence

47. Shackleford, Holly. Phone and email correspondence. Charlotte County Extension.

48. Steward, Mary. Email correspondence

49. "The Effect of Soil Saturation on Trees and Other Plants". Hillsborough County Extension Service, Seffner, FL., University of Florida IFAS Extension.

50. Wacker, Don. Email correspondence

51. Watkins, Teresa. University of Florida/IFAS, Florida Yards and Neighborhoods for Lake, Orange, and Seminole County. Email correspondence. 2004.

52. Williams, Jeff, email correspondence.

53. Williams, Larry. University of Florida Extension Agent. Okaloosa County. Email correspondence.

54. Williams, Sherry. "Hurricanes Charley, Francis, and Jeanne: Their Effects on Brevard County's Landscape". Brevard County Department of Natural Resources. 2004

Index

* See "Easy Gardens for Florida"
* See "Best Garden Color for Florida"

These two books are volumes one and two of this series, also by Pamela Crawford.

Index

Index

* See "Easy Gardens for Florida"
* See "Best Garden Color for Florida"

These two books are volumes one and two of this series, also by Pamela Crawford.

Syzigium cumini 74

T

Tabebuia 31, 55, 89
Tabebuia caraiba, * *
Tabebuia impetiginosa *
Tabebuia ipe *
Tabebuia ssp. 89
Tabernaemontana spp., *
Tagetes spp. *
Tallow, Chinese 89
Tamarind, Wild 89
Tangerine 89
Taxodium ascendens 68
Taxodium distichum 67, 68
Tecoma stans *
Tecomanthe venusta, See Pink Petticoat
Tecomaria capensis, See Cape Honeysuckle
Thespesia populnea 75
Thrinax radiata * 83
Thryallis, * * 89
Thuja occidentalis 63
Thunbergia alata *
Thunbergia erecta *
Thunbergia grandiflora *
Ti 90
Ti 'Black Magic' *
Ti 'Purple Prince' *
Ti Red Sister, * *
Ti Sherbert *
Ti Tricolor *
Tibouchina compacta *
Tibouchina granulosa *
Torenia fournieri *
Trachelospermum jasminoides, *
Tradescantia pallida 'Purpurea', see Purple Queen 85
Trial gardens *
Trimezia martinicensis, *
Trimming *
Trinette, *
Tropical Sage *
Tropical Snowball *
Tropical Wisteria, *
Turk's Cap *
Turnera subulata *
Twelve Apostle's Plant *

U

Ulmus parvifolia 68

V

Variegated Arboricola, *

Variegated Liriope, *
Variegated Peperomia *
Variegated Ginger *
Verbena spp. *
Viburnum, Walters 90
Viburnum obovatum 90
Viola x Wittrockiana *
Vireya *

W

Walking Iris, *
Washingtonia robusta 83
Water efficiently, *
Watering, establishment, *
Watering, *
Water Oak, See Oak, Water
Wax Begonia *
Wax Myrtle
Wedelia trilobata *
Weeding, *
West Indian Shower *
White Alder *
White Begonia, see *Begonia odorata alba*
White Bird of Paradise, *
Wild Coffee 90
Wisteria, Tropical, *
Wodyetia bifucata * 81

X

Xanthostemon chrysanthus 70

Y

Yellow Elder *
Yellow Lantana *
Yellow Mussaenda, *
Yellow Tabebuia, *
Yesterday, Today, and Tomorrow, see *Brunfelsia grandiflora* * 90
Ylang-Ylang 32, 90, 147

Z

Zamia furfuracea 79
Zanthoxylum fagara 74
Zone information * 5
Zinnia spp. *

The Florida Gardening Series is a set of books designed to make Florida gardening easier.

Volume 1 - "Easy Gardens for South Florida"

This book is the first of a series of books designed to educate both gardeners - and the professionals who work with them - about the keys to achieving an easy, beautiful landscape. It describes in detail the first (and easiest) 100 plants that survived decades of extensive trials and includes chapters on garden planting and maintenance that are critical for the success of the Florida garden. It tells you how to water, plant, fertilize, control pests, mulch, trim, and control weeds. These maintenance instructions will keep people from making all the mistakes the author made when she began gardening here. She shares years of research and experience that should save you years of mistakes and frustration.

Volume 2 - "Best Garden Color for Florida"

"Best Garden Color for Florida" is a must-have for Florida gardeners and professionals who love garden color! It is not only loaded with 575 spectacular photos, but also includes reams of easy-to-understand information about use and care of 150 terrific Florida plants. The plant information is complemented with chapters filled with ideas about color for butterflies, sun, shade, salt, and wind.
The book is a result of decades of plant research by the author to determine which plants and planting strategies give the most color for the least amount of care. The author personally grew most of the plants, giving her practical experience with all aspects of the plants' use and maintenance. It is a companion to the bestselling "Easy Gardens for South Florida". No information is repeated in either book. The two work together to give you the best garden color for Florida.

Volume 4 - "Containers Gardens for Florida "

Container Gardens for Florida

This book is currently being written for release in early 2005. From the author: "I used container gardens in my landscape design business for over 10 years, and I spent the last year working exclusively on container gardens as research for this book. I have tested thousands of plants and hundreds of containers to learn which ones give the best performance with the least amount of care. I have especially looked for methods of using containers for maximum design impact, like the huge hanging baskets I've seen in England. After my usual number of early failures, I have had some great successes, and am very excited about this book. It not only covers the best plants and containers but also great methods of designing with these containers in your garden.

See our Web site at www.easygardencolor.com for more information about our books.